全国高等卫生职业教育创新型人才培养"十三五"规划教材

供医学美容技术等专业使用

实用美容英语会话

English Conversations of Cosmetology

主　审	操时尧
主　编	张卫华　余芊芊
副主编	熊　蕊　徐红莉　杨美文　程跃英
编　者	温中梅　梁超兰　李文娟　张　颖

华中科技大学出版社
http://www.hustp.com
中国·武汉

内 容 简 介

本书为全国高等卫生职业教育创新型人才培养"十三五"规划教材。

本书将美容职业活动分为美容专业与美容院的初步认识、化妆品简介、美容前台英语会话、美容顾问英语会话、美容师英语会话、美体师英语会话、化妆师和美甲师英语会话共7个单元,每个单元再分为2~3个任务,每个任务包括热身活动、实践活动和拓展活动3个部分。

本书供医学美容技术、美容美体艺术、人物形象设计等专业使用。

图书在版编目(CIP)数据

实用美容英语会话/张卫华,余芊芊主编. —武汉:华中科技大学出版社,2017.8
 全国高等卫生职业教育创新型人才培养"十三五"规划教材. 医学美容技术专业
 ISBN 978-7-5680-3233-9

Ⅰ.①实… Ⅱ.①张… ②余… Ⅲ.①美容-服务业-英语-高等职业教育-教材 Ⅳ.①F719.9

中国版本图书馆 CIP 数据核字(2017)第 188096 号

实用美容英语会话 张卫华 余芊芊 主编
Shiyong Meirong Yingyu Huihua

策划编辑:居　颖
责任编辑:秦　曌
封面设计:原色设计
责任校对:张会军
责任监印:周治超
出版发行:华中科技大学出版社(中国·武汉)　　电话:(027)81321913
　　　　　武汉市东湖新技术开发区华工科技园　　邮编:430223
录　　排:华中科技大学惠友文印中心
印　　刷:武汉科源印刷设计有限公司
开　　本:787mm×1092mm　1/16
印　　张:7.75
字　　数:197千字
版　　次:2017年8月第1版第1次印刷
定　　价:38.00元

本书若有印装质量问题,请向出版社营销中心调换
全国免费服务热线:400-6679-118　　竭诚为您服务
版权所有　侵权必究

全国高等卫生职业教育创新型人才培养"十三五"规划教材（医学美容技术专业）编委会

委　员（按姓氏笔画排序）

申芳芳	山东中医药高等专科学校	周　围	宜春职业技术学院
付　莉	郑州铁路职业技术学院	周丽艳	江西医学高等专科学校
孙　晶	白城医学高等专科学校	周建军	重庆三峡医药高等专科学校
杨加峰	宁波卫生职业技术学院	赵　丽	辽宁医药职业学院
杨家林	鄂州职业大学	赵自然	吉林大学白求恩第一医院
邱子津	重庆医药高等专科学校	晏志勇	江西卫生职业学院
何　伦	东南大学	徐毓华	江苏建康职业学院
陈丽君	皖北卫生职业学院	黄丽娃	长春医学高等专科学校
陈丽超	铁岭卫生职业学院	韩银淑	厦门医学院
陈景华	黑龙江中医药大学佳木斯学院	蔡成功	沧州医学高等专科学校
武　燕	安徽中医药高等专科学校	谭　工	重庆三峡医药高等专科学校
周　羽	盐城卫生职业技术学院	熊　蕊	湖北职业技术学院

前言
QIANYAN

美容护理的目标不仅是让人们在外貌上更加年轻、美丽,而且通过按摩、指压、芳疗 SPA 等自然养生疗法使人们在身体和精神上释放压力,让每一个走进美容院的人都充满自信,拥有乐观、积极的心态,自觉关注自己的身体状况,努力提高生活质量,从而达到人与社会的和谐。

随着美容市场的不断规范和成熟,不仅需要技术娴熟的美容技师,而且需要具备一定美容专业知识和良好沟通能力的美容咨询师和美容顾问,更需要能适应国内外市场需求、具备国际眼光的战略性人才。英语是当今世界应用广泛的语言之一,学好英语自然为他们开启了一扇通往国际市场的大门。因此,我们不仅要在课堂上教授学生美容理论知识和技能,在实战中提升他们的营销和沟通能力,更要鼓励学生学好英语,拓展学生的眼界,为他们将来实现职场理想奠定坚实的基础。

《实用美容英语会话》根据国家制订的高级美容师职业资格要求编写,是一本美容相关专业的英语教材,也适用于中高级美容师的职业培训。本书具有以下几个特点。

(1) 凸显"以职业为导向,以技能为核心"的指导思想。本书按照美容师、美体师、化妆师和美甲师等美容专业从业人员和美容前台、美容顾问和咨询师等职业岗位群为线索,以美容院工作过程为导向,培养美容师与客户及同事用英语进行日常会话和专业交流的能力。

(2) 情境教学,强调职业针对性。本书将美容职业活动分为美容专业与美容院的初步认识、化妆品简介、美容前台英语会话、美容顾问英语会话、美容师英语会话、美体师英语会话、化妆师和美甲师英语会话共 7 个单元,每个单元再分为 2~3 个任务,每个任务包括热身活动、实践活动和拓展活动 3 个部分。本书力求突出美容职业培训的特色,达到英语语言运用能力和美容专业知识学习并举的目的。

(3) 真实话题,增强专业指导性。实践活动以美容真实话题为会话素材,训练在该任务下需要掌握的专业词汇和句型,强调不同分工的美容师日常英语话题表达的特定性。

(4) 图文并茂,提高图书趣味性。热身活动是与任务相关的专业词汇的学习和运用,为避免单纯词汇和语法学习的枯燥和乏味感,我们下载和拍摄了大量相关图片供学生认读,并在会话和练习等部分也配有相关图片,以提高学生学习的兴趣和积极性。

(5) 互动设计,追求课堂实用性。拓展部分学习日常英语经典表达,通过学生结对练习来提高英语口语水平。

(6) 内容丰富,促进教学自主性。对于英语基础较好、有兴趣进一步提高英语语言能力的学生和读者,我们提供了部分中英文对照的涉及美容知识的短文,设计了一些问题供阅读后思考。同时,在每个单元后面提供了一些美容的网站供学生和读者进行自主学习。

　　本教材的编写得到我校美容学院领导的大力支持及美容教研室老师们的热心指导,在此一并表示衷心感谢,并感谢操时尧教授在审定英语会话上提供的帮助。本教材的出版要特别致谢东方美美容院协助拍摄和华中科技大学出版社有限责任公司的编辑们的慷慨赐教。

　　由于编者水平有限,书中难免出现疏漏和缺憾,恳请教材使用者批评指正,以帮助我们再版时改进。

张卫华　余芊芊

目录

第一单元　美容专业与美容院的初步认识
Unit One　Introduction to Cosmetology and Beauty Salon / 1
　　任务一　美容专业和工作岗位
　　Task One　Majors of Cosmetology and Future Jobs / 1
　　任务二　美容院的初步认识
　　Task Two　Modern Beauty Salon / 6

第二单元　化妆品简介
Unit Two　Introduction to Cosmetics / 12
　　任务一　化妆品的分类和辨识
　　Task One　Classification and Identification of Cosmetics / 12
　　任务二　防晒品标志
　　Task Two　Labels on the Sunscreens / 18

第三单元　美容前台英语会话
Unit Three　Oral English for Beauty Receptionist / 23
　　任务一　第一次预约
　　Task One　The First Appointment / 23
　　任务二　电话预约和回访
　　Task Two　Phone Appointment and Post-service Interview / 27

第四单元　美容顾问英语会话
Unit Four　Oral English for Beauty Adviser / 33
　　任务一　到店服务
　　Task One　Service in the Beauty Salon / 33
　　任务二　客户交流
　　Task Two　Communication with Clients / 37
　　任务三　居家护理指导
　　Task Three　Home Treatment Guide / 43

第五单元　美容师英语会话
Unit Five　Oral English for Beautician / 48
　　任务一　皮肤的种类和问题
　　Task One　Types of Skin and Skin Problems / 48
　　任务二　面部护理
　　Task Two　Facial Care / 54

　　　　　　任务三　眼部护理
　　　　　　Task Three　Eye Care　　　　　　　　　　　　　　　　/ 60

第六单元　美体师英语会话
Unit Six　Oral English for Body Therapist　　　　　　　　　　　/ 66
　　　　　　任务一　头颈部护理
　　　　　　Task One　Head and Neck Care　　　　　　　　　　　/ 66
　　　　　　任务二　背部护理
　　　　　　Task Two　Back Care　　　　　　　　　　　　　　　/ 71
　　　　　　任务三　水疗法
　　　　　　Task Three　SPA　　　　　　　　　　　　　　　　　/ 78

第七单元　化妆师和美甲师英语会话
Unit Seven　Oral English for Cosmetician and Manicurist　　　　/ 88
　　　　　　任务一　日妆
　　　　　　Task One　Daily Make-up　　　　　　　　　　　　　/ 88
　　　　　　任务二　新娘妆
　　　　　　Task Two　Bridal Make-up　　　　　　　　　　　　　/ 93
　　　　　　任务三　美甲
　　　　　　Task Three　Manicure　　　　　　　　　　　　　　　/ 100

附录A　常见外国女性的名字
Appendix A　Common foreign females' name　　　　　　　　　/ 107
附录B　中外节日英汉对照
Appendix B　Chinese and Foreign Festivals　　　　　　　　　　/ 112
附录C　背景知识和网站链接
Appendix C　Background Information and Web Links　　　　　/ 114
参考文献
References　　　　　　　　　　　　　　　　　　　　　　　/ 116

第一单元 美容专业与美容院的初步认识
Unit One Introduction to Cosmetology and Beauty Salon

任务一 美容专业和工作岗位
Task One Majors of Cosmetology and Future Jobs

图 1-1

Ⅰ. 热身活动
Ⅰ. Warm up Activities

A. Learn professional words and expressions.

Cosmetic Professionals

beautician[bjuˈtiʃən]	n. 美容师
cosmetician/make-up artist	化妆师
hair stylist[ˈstailist]	发型师,美发师
therapist[ˈθerəpist]	n. 理疗师
aroma therapist	芳疗师
SPA beauty therapist	水疗师
manicurist[ˈmænikjuərist]	n. 美甲师
beauty adviser/consultant	美容顾问/咨询师

beauty director/manager　　　　　　　　　美容店长/经理

B. Look at these pictures and point out what their jobs are.

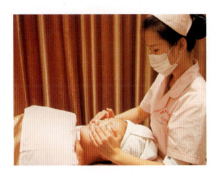

图 1-2

图 1-3

图 1-4

图 1-5

图 1-6

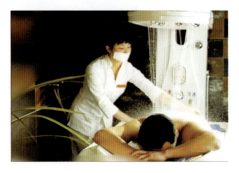

图 1-7

Conversation 1.1

Cosmetic Majors and Future Jobs

Mary: Hi, Anna. It's nearly half past seven. Let's go, hurry up.

Anna: All right. Today is the first day when we become college students. I'm very glad we'll meet some new classmates and teachers.

Mary: Yes, we were in the same high school and now we are so lucky to be arranged in the same dormitory in the college. I wonder if we could meet some other old friends.

图 1-8

Anna: I would like to make some new friends.

Joanna: Hello, are you Mary? Do you remember me? We were schoolmates in Sunny High School.

Mary: Oh, yes, you are Joanna. Long time no see. Anna, this is my old friend, Joanna.

Joanna: Nice to meet you, Anna. I'm Joanna.

Anna: Nice to meet you too. What's your major?

Joanna: I'm a freshman majoring in medical cosmetic technology. What about you?

图 1-9

图 1-10

Mary: Oh, we three are in the same department. (Cheers!) I major in Beauty Education and Management. Anna majors in Traditional Chinese Medicine Healthcare.

Anna: Traditional Chinese Medicine Healthcare is my major. I want to be a skilled body therapist.

Joanna: I dream to be a beautician in a large SPA chamber. Mary, what would you like to be in the future?

Mary: I want to be a beauty adviser helping run beauty shops.

Anna: Do you intend to have your own beauty salon?

Mary: Oh, maybe. I'll consider it if I get rich experience in management and earn enough money for a beauty salon.

Joanna: Wish you make it one day!

Mary: Thank you. Oh, it's about time to have classes. Let's go.

New Words and Expressions

major['meidʒə]	n. 专业 v. 主修 adj. 主要的
freshman['freʃmən]	n. (中学或大学的)一年级新生
cosmetology[ˌkɔzmə'tɔlədʒi]	n. 整容术,美容术,美容学
cosmetics[kɔz'metiks]	n. 化妆品
technology[tek'nɔlədʒi]	n. 技术,科技
department[di'pɑːtmənt]	n. 系,部门,科室
client['klaiənt]	n. 顾客,客户
major in	以……为专业
Medical Cosmetic Technology	医学美容技术
Beauty Education & Management	美容教育与管理
Traditional Chinese Medicine Healthcare	传统中医养生
make it	及时到达,(非正式)成功

Ⅱ. 实践活动
Ⅱ. Practical Activities

A. Read the conversation 1.1 and then fill the table below.

Name	Major	Future job
Mary		
	Traditional Chinese Medicine Healthcare	
		a beautician

B. Read in pairs and mark the statements True (T) or False (F).

(　) 1. Mary and Joanna are old friends since high school.
(　) 2. These three girls were classmates in middle school.
(　) 3. They are in the same major.
(　) 4. Joanna's major is Traditional Chinese Medicine Healthcare.
(　) 5. Anna wants to be a body therapist.

C. Fill in the missing words.

1. I'm very glad we'll meet some new _____ _____ _____.
   我很高兴会认识一些新的老师和同学。

2. We were in the same high school and we are so _____ to be arranged in the same dormitory in the college.
   我们是高中同学,很幸运,上大学又分在同一间宿舍。

3. I _____ _____ _____ make some new friends.
   我想认识一些新朋友。

4. _____ _____ _____ _____. Anna, this is my old friend, Joanna.
   好久不见。安娜，这是我的好朋友，乔安娜。

5. Nice to meet you. What's your _____?
   很高兴认识你，你是学什么专业的？

D. Translate the following sentences into English.

1. 我是医学美容技术专业的一年级学生。我们都是一个系的——美容健康系。
2. 我主修美容教育与管理专业。安娜主修传统中医养生专业。
3. 我想做一名技术熟练的理疗师，可以去一家大型SPA会所工作。
4. 我想做一名美容顾问，帮助经理管理店务。
5. 如果我有丰富的管理经验和足够的资金，我会考虑自己开店。

Ⅲ. 拓展活动
Ⅲ. Extension Activities

Read typical expressions on Greetings and Introduction and then practice in pairs.

图 1-11

Greetings and Introduction

1. —Hello/Hi!
   嗨！
   —Oh, it's you! The world is so small. Pleased to meet you.
   是你呀，这个世界太小了。很高兴见到你。

2. Good morning/afternoon/evening.
   早上/下午/晚上好。

3. —What's up?
   最近怎么样？/有什么新鲜事发生吗？
   —Nothing new. /Not much.
   老样子。/没什么。

4. —How's everything going?
   一切还好吧？

—Long time no see. Everything goes well, thanks.

好久不见。都好，谢谢。

5. —How have you been?

   近来过得怎么样？

   —Not bad.

   还不错。

6. —How are you doing?

   你好吗？

   —I'm fine/very well, thank you. And you?

   还好，谢谢，你呢？

   —I'm fine, thanks.

   我很好，谢谢。

7. —Nice to meet you.

   很高兴见到你。

   —Nice to meet you, too.

   见到你我也很高兴。

8. May I know your name?

   我可以知道你的名字吗？

9. Let me introduce myself.

   让我做个自我介绍。

10. —Could you introduce me to Mr. Smith?

    你能介绍我认识史密斯先生吗？

    —It's my honor /pleasure to introduce.

    非常荣幸/乐意。

任务二　美容院的初步认识
Task Two　Modern Beauty Salon

图 1-12

Ⅰ. 热身活动
Ⅰ. Warm up Activities

A. Learn professional words and expressions.

Common Service Programs

facial treatment/care	面部护理
body care	身体护理
aromatherapy[ˌærəməˈθɛrəpi]	n. 芳香疗法
SPA beauty treatment	SPA 美疗
manicure[ˈmænɪˌkjuə]	n. 美甲
make up	化妆
hairdressing	n. 美发

B. Match cosmetic professionals in the left column with service programs in the right column.

	Cosmetic professionals		Service programs
1	beautician	A	SPA treatment and hydrotherapy
2	cosmetician	B	provide hair dye and perm
3	hair stylist	C	manicure
4	aroma therapist	D	provide all kinds of make-up
5	SPA beauty therapist	E	provide skin care
6	manicurist	F	provide aromatherapy

Conversation 1.2

Visiting Angel Beauty Salon

图 1-13

A teacher takes several students to visit Angel Beauty Salon. The beauty receptionist Betty and the beauty adviser Mary are receiving them.

Betty: Hello, welcome to Angel Beauty Salon. I'm Betty, the beauty receptionist.

Teacher: Hello, Betty, would you like to show us around your beauty salon?

Betty: It would be my pleasure. Now, we're in the reception room. Our clients can take a rest and discuss their needs with our beauty adviser as well.

Student 1: Oh, it's decorated just like a four-star hotel. It feels very relaxing to be in such a delightful ambiance.

图 1-14

Betty: Yes, you said it.

Student 2: I'm willing to work in such a comfortable environment from the bottom of my heart.

Teacher: Very well. This is one of the reasons why I show you this beauty salon.

Betty: Excuse me, I have to answer a phone call. Mary will continue to show you around our beauty salon.

Mary: Hello, I'm Mary, a beauty adviser. This way, please. This is the batching room for preparing materials.

Student 3: Great! Wow, you have a disinfection cabinet here.

Mary: Yes, our disinfection cabinet is generally used to disinfect used items such as towels, bath towels and sheets.

Student 3: That certainly makes the customer feel at ease.

Mary: Absolutely!

Student 1: Wow, you see, the crystal lamp on the ceiling is so beautiful! And the mirror in front of the dressing table is really big!

Mary: Thank you for your compliment. All of the interior decorations are carefully chosen by our salon manager. We not only want to help bring out the beauty and good health in every client, but also would like to make the client feel well pampered. Clients will dress themselves up here. If necessary, we also provide make-up and manicure. Of course, there are additional service fees for that. This way, please.

图 1-15

图 1-16

Student 2: Are these all beauty treatment rooms? How many beds are there in your salon?

Mary: Um, 25 beds. There are five three-bed and four double-bed rooms. We also have two single rooms that are specially designed for our VIP clients.

Student 1: What service programs do you offer?

Mary: The most common programs are facial care and body care. Besides, we also offer other services such as aromatherapy, SPA beauty treatment and hydrotherapy, various make-up and manicure. All of our beauticians have got vocational beautician certificates.

图 1-17

Student 3: It's not easy to be a qualified beautician. I have to study hard to pass the National Beautician Vocational Skill Examination.

Mary: May your dreams come true.

Students: Thank you very much!

Mary: Not at all!

New Words and Expressions

angel [ˈeindʒəl]　　　　　　　　　n. 天使，天使般的人
salon [səˈlɔn]　　　　　　　　　　n. 客厅，沙龙

decorate ['dekəreit]　　　　　　　　v. 装饰，布置，装修
relaxation ['rilæk'seʃən]　　　　　n. 放松，消遣，松弛
elegant ['eligənt]　　　　　　　　adj. 优雅的，雅致的
comfortable ['kʌmfətəbl]　　　　 adj. 舒适，安逸，安慰
environment [in'vairənmənt]　　 n. 环境，外界，周围
charge [tʃɑ:dʒ]　　　　　　　　　vt. 要价 n. 责任，费用
double ['dʌbl]　　　　　　　　　adj. 双重的，成双的
beauty salon / shop　　　　　　 美容院
reception room　　　　　　　　 接待室，接待区
dressing table　　　　　　　　　梳妆台
batching room　　　　　　　　　配料间
show around　　　　　　　　　　带（某人）参观

Ⅱ. 实践活动
Ⅱ. Practical Activities

A. Read in pairs and mark the statements True (T) or False (F).

(　) 1. Today we'll visit Angel beauty Salon so that we can work there.
(　) 2. Betty is a beauty adviser.
(　) 3. Clients can have a talk with the beauty adviser in the reception room.
(　) 4. Services such as make-up and manicure are free in Angel Beauty Salon.
(　) 5. It is very easy to be a qualified beautician.

B. Fill in the missing words.

1. Hello, welcome to Angel Beauty Salon. I'm Betty, the _____ _____.
   大家好！欢迎光临安琪儿美容院。我是美容前台接待，贝蒂。

2. Betty, would you like to _____ _____ _____ your salon?
   贝蒂，可以带我们参观一下你们店吗？

3. Now, we're in the _____ _____.
   我们现在是在接待室。

4. I'm willing to work in such a comfortable environment from _____ _____ _____ my heart.
   我发自内心地愿意在这种舒适的环境中工作。

5. This is one of the reasons _____ I show you to this beauty salon.
   这就是我带你们来参观的原因之一。

C. Translate the following sentences into English.

1. 我是玛丽，是这儿的美容顾问。请走这边，这是一间配料室。
2. 这儿装修得真是豪华，看上去就像四星级酒店一样。
3. 顾客接受服务完毕后会自己在这梳妆，如果需要，我们也提供化妆和美甲服务。
4. 我们有五个三人间和四个两人间。还有两间精装修的单人间，是为 VIP 客户准备的。

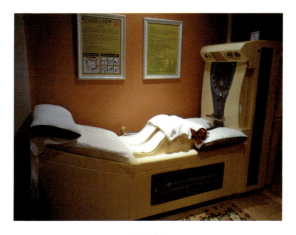

图 1-18

5. 最常见的项目是皮肤护理和各种身体护理,此外还有香薰疗法、SPA 美疗和水疗法、化妆与造型和美甲服务。

Ⅲ. 拓展活动
Ⅲ. Extension Activities

Read typical expressions on Likes and Dislikes then practice in pairs.

图 1-19

图 1-20

Likes and Dislikes

1. I like making up.
   我喜欢化妆。
2. I hate very spicy food.
   我不喜欢太辣的食物。
3. I'm crazy about shrimps.
   我非常喜欢吃虾。
4. I'm fond of light music.
   我喜欢轻音乐。
5. I can't stand his behavior.
   我受不了他的举止。

第二单元 化妆品简介
Unit Two Introduction to Cosmetics

任务一 化妆品的分类和辨识
Task One Classification and Identification of Cosmetics

图 2-1

Ⅰ. 热身活动
Ⅰ. Warm up Activities

A. Learn professional words and expressions.

Types of Cosmetics

paste[peist]	n. 膏
powder['paudə]	n. 粉
oil	n. 油
cream	n. 霜
lotion	n. 乳液
gel	n. 啫喱
cleansing products	清洁品
skin care products	护肤品

decoration cosmetics　　　　　　　　修饰用化妆品

B. Identify the following brands of cosmetics. What are your favorite brands? What other brands do you like?

图 2-2　　　　　　　　　　　　　图 2-3

图 2-4　　　　　　　　　　　　　图 2-5

图 2-6　　　　　　　　　　　　　图 2-7

图 2-8　　　　　　　　　　　　　图 2-9

Conversation 2.1

Identifying Cosmetics

Eliza—a client　　Mary—a beauty adviser

Eliza: There are large categories of cosmetics, how do you divide them?

Mary: Well, according to the shape, cosmetics can be divided into lotion, oil, cream, paste

图 2-10

and powder. We can also divide them into three types by effects: cleansing products, skin care products and decoration cosmetics.

Eliza: I used to buy some cheap cosmetics at night market, which caused my skin red and swollen. Where are proper places for me to buy cosmetics?

Mary: You'd better buy cosmetics in department stores, specialty counters, open-shelf specialty stores and well-established direct selling channels. Some famous brands are rather expensive but their quality is guaranteed and they have better services. Many brand products are on sale during holidays.

图 2-11

Eliza: I see. I doubt that these discounted cosmetics are of good quality.

Mary: You can identify the quality by checking the label on the container about the description, ingredients, usage, manufacturer and importer, especially manufacture date and expiry date.

Eliza: How can we tell if it has gone bad?

Mary: First, you can check if its color changes. Second, see if there is any shape change like a layer of oil on top of the cream. Finally, the smell can tell you whether a product is fresh.

Eliza: Should I choose cosmetics with a strong scent or not?

Mary: It depends. If your skin is sensitive or you have any allergy, the best choice is to stay away from scented products. Therefore, you'd better know your skin quality.

Eliza: Thank you for telling me the detailed information about cosmetics.

Mary: You're welcome.

图 2-12

New Words and Expressions

classification[ˌklæsifiˈkeiʃən]	n. 分类,类别
identification[aiˌdentifiˈkeiʃən]	n. 确认
cleanse[klenz]	v. 使……清洁,净化
guarantee[ˌgærənˈti]	v. 保证 n. 保证,担保
discounted[ˈdiskauntid]	adj. 已打折的
ingredient[inˈgri:diənt]	n. 成分,原料,配料
manufacture[ˌmænjuˈfæktʃə]	v. 制造 n. 制造,制造业
preservation[ˌprezəˈveiʃən]	n. 保存,维护,防腐
layer[ˈleiə]	n. 层 v. 分层
scent[sent]	n. 气味,香味
artificial[ˌɑ:tiˈfiʃəl]	adj. 人造的,虚伪的
fragrance[ˈfreigrəns]	n. 香味
allergy[ˈælədʒi]	n. 过敏症
complicated[ˈkɔmplikeitid]	adj. 复杂的
preservative[priˈzə:vətiv]	n. 防腐剂
specialty counter	专柜
open-shelf specialty store	开架式专卖店
well-established direct selling channels	畅通的直销渠道
on sale	促销,甩卖
expiry date	过期日期

Ⅱ. 实践活动
Ⅱ. Practical Activities

A. **Read the conversation and then mark the statements True (T) or False (F).**

(　) 1. Cosmetics can be classified according to their shape and effect.

(　) 2. We can buy cosmetics in night market because it's very cheap.

(　) 3. We shouldn't buy discounted cosmetics because they have gone bad.

(　) 4. We can check the label on the container to identify the quality of cosmetics.

(　) 5. We can tell the quality of cosmetics by checking its color, smell and taste.

B. Fill in the missing words.

1. Cosmetics can be divided into _____, _____, _____, paste and powder according to the shape.
   根据形状化妆品可以分为乳液、油状、霜状、膏状和粉状。

2. Some famous brands are rather _____ but their quality is guaranteed and they have better _____.
   一些著名的品牌价格有些贵但是质量有保证,且有较好的服务。

3. I doubt that these discounted cosmetics _____ _____ _____ _____.
   我想知道这些打折的化妆品是否质量有保证。

4. How can you tell if it _____ _____ _____?
   你怎么辨别变质产品?

5. You'd better know your _____ _____.
   你最好了解自己皮肤的性质。

C. Translate the following sentences into English.

1. 根据用途化妆品可以分为清洁品、护肤品和修饰用化妆品。
2. 你最好去百货商店、专卖柜台、开架式的专卖店或者比较好的直销渠道买化妆品。
3. 你可以查看标签上的产品说明、成分、用法、厂商和进口商,特别是通过生产日期、有效期和保存方法来辨别质量。
4. 首先看颜色是否有变化,第二看形状是否有变化,最后闻气味看产品是否是新鲜的。
5. 如果你是敏感肌肤或过敏体质,最好不要用香味很浓的产品。

图 2-13

Ⅲ. 拓展活动
Ⅲ. Extension Activities

A. Read typical expressions on Gratitude and then practice in pairs.

Gratitude

1. Thanks for your help.
   谢谢你的帮助。
2. You're welcome.
   不要客气。
3. You've been a big help.
   你帮了大忙了。
4. I can't express how grateful I was.
   我无法表达我的感激之情。
5. Thank you for everything you've done.
   谢谢你为我做的一切。

B. Read the passage and then complete the following exercises.

Learn to Read Cosmetics Label

图 2-14

The label represents the identification of a product. In order to choose cosmetics that are safe and secure, we must carefully read and understand the labels.

1. Product name   We can know the function from the name of the product. For example, "moisturizing lotion" can moisturize skin with abundant water.

2. Ingredients   Net contents are listed here. For example, in a bottle of perfume, purified water, fragrance and alcohol are common ingredients.

3. Directions   Under directions we can find information regarding how and where to apply the products as well as expected outcomes after application.

4. Period of validity   Sometimes the expiration date is not provided and there is only a manufacturing date and the period of validity. We can figure out the expiration date by adding the period of validity to the manufacturing date.

5. Manufacturing date   It refers to the date when the product is produced.

6. Preservation   Improper preservation may cause quality change. First, cosmetics

usually must be stored in a cool, dry place, if put into the bathroom, its quality may change easily, especially some products with natural ingredients. Second, direct sun exposure should be avoided. Third, bottles must be kept tightly closed after each application. Fourth, some products with vitamin C must be stored in the refrigerator to avoid becoming bad. Don't put some products stored in the refrigerator to expose outside for too long time. Fifth, if the product is too much, you can divide them into several small containers. Sixth, you'd better take products with a little stick instead of your hand directly.

7. Name and address of the supplier　The manufacturer's name and address are listed here. If the product is imported, the information regarding the importer's name and address should be provided.

Match column A—Information on Labels with column B—Chinese Meaning.

A　Information on Labels	B　Chinese Meaning
1.　product name	a.　有效日期
2.　ingredient	b.　品名
3.　manufacturing date	c.　使用说明
4.　effective date	d.　专利号
5.　period of validity	e.　成分
6.　expiration date	f.　盎司
7.　name and address of the supplier	g.　制造日期
8.　directions	h.　有效期
9.　preservation	i.　保存方法
10.　patent Nos.	j.　到期日
11.　ounce (OZ.)	k.　永久性生活产品
12.　forever living products	l.　供应商名称和地址

任务二　防晒品标志
Task Two　Labels on the Sunscreens

图 2-15

Ⅰ. 热身活动
Ⅰ. Warm up Activities

A. Learn professional words and expressions.

Sun Protection Cosmetics

sunscreen['sʌnskriːn]	n. 防晒霜
sunburn['sʌnbɜːn]	n. 晒伤,晒黑
suntan['sʌntæn]	n. 皮肤晒黑
ultraviolet（UV）rays	紫外线
sun protection factor(SPF)	防晒系数
sun-locking cream/sunblocking cream/sunproof cream	防晒霜
sunblock/BB cream/sun block/day protector/UV protector	隔离霜

B. Look at these pictures and point out what they are.

图 2-16　　　　　图 2-17　　　　　图 2-18　　　　　图 2-19

Conversation 2.2

Meanings of Labels on the Sunscreen

图 2-20

Eliza—a client　　Mary—a beauty adviser

Mary: Where are you going to spend this summer vacation?

Eliza: I am going to Hawaii.

Mary: Sounds good. You'd better take care of your skin with proper sunscreen while going out.

Eliza: Mm, I have heard that ultraviolet (UV) rays are very intensive there. Do they hurt people's skin?

Mary: Of course. Sun shine contains three types of ultraviolet (UV) rays: UVA, UVB and UVC. UVA is of long waves and it penetrates objects easily. It can cause sunburn, suntan and aging. UVB is of short waves and it can cause skin red and swollen as well as blistering and peeling. UVC is of shorter waves and it may cause skin cancer.

图 2-21

Eliza: Oh, it's terrible. I know that there are some symbols on the labels of sunscreens such as SPF15, SPF30, PA^+, PA^{++} and PA^{+++}. What do these labels mean?

Mary: SPF refers to sun protection factor, which prevents your skin from sunburn. One SPF equals 15 minutes. For instance, SPF15 means that the expected sun protection time is 15(SPF) × 15 (minutes) = 225 minutes of sun protection. The PA value indicates UVA parameter. A^+ means that the suntan effects are to put off two to four times, A^{++} means four to eight times, and A^{+++} over eight times.

Eliza: Oh, can you tell me what the differences between sunscreen and sunblock?

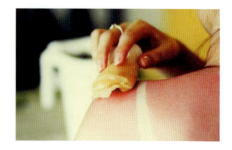

图 2-22　　　　　　　　　图 2-23

Mary: Sunscreen and sunblock are both excellent forms of sun protection. Some people are sensitive or allergic to certain ingredients in sunscreens. Choosing between the two is a matter of personal preference and necessity. As long as you choose an SPF of at least 30 in summer, you are providing adequate protection for your skin. If you go swimming or do other water sports, you will be exposed to the sun for very long time and hence you need to use sun protector whose SPF is higher than 30. Wish you have cool holidays.

Eliza: Thank you so much.

Mary: My pleasure.

图 2-24

图 2-25

New Words and Expressions

Hawaii [hɑːˈwaiiː]	n. 夏威夷（美国州名）
intensive [inˈtensiv]	adj. 密集的，强烈的，精细的
ultraviolet [ˌʌltrəˈvaiəlit]	adj. 紫外线的 n. 紫外线
rays [reiz]	n. 射线
penetrate [ˈpenətreit]	v. 渗透，看穿，穿透
aging [ˈeidʒiŋ]	n. 老化，衰老
swollen [ˈswəulən]	adj. 肿胀的
blister [ˈblistə]	n. 水泡 vi. 生水疱
peel [piːl]	v. 剥落，起皮 n. 水果皮，蔬菜皮
cancer [ˈkænsə]	n. 癌，肿瘤，毒瘤
parameter [pəˈræmitə]	n. 参量，参数
hence [hens]	adv. 因此，从此以后

Ⅱ. 实践活动
Ⅱ. Practical Activities

A. Read the conversation and then mark the statements True (T) or False (F).

( ) 1. Sun shine contains three types of ultraviolet (UV) rays.

( ) 2. UVA is of very short waves and it may cause skin cancer.

( ) 3. UVB is of long waves and it penetrates objects easily.

( ) 4. SPF15 means that the expected sun protection time is 225 minutes.

( ) 5. A$^+$ means that the sun-tan effects are to put off two times.

B. Fill the meaning of following symbols on the sunscreen in English.

Symbols	Meanings in English
UVA	
UVB	
UVC	
SPF	

续表

Symbols	Meanings in English
SPF15	
PA⁺	
PA⁺⁺	
PA⁺⁺⁺	

C. Translate the following sentences into English.

1. 你外出时最好用些防晒霜保护好你的皮肤。
2. 太阳光包括三种紫外线：UVA、UVB 和 UVC。UVA 是长波，能轻易穿透皮肤，会造成晒斑、皮肤晒黑和老化。
3. UVB 是短波，它能造成脱皮、皮肤红肿和水疱。UVC 波长更短，可能诱发皮肤癌。
4. SPF 指的是防晒系数，可以预防皮肤产生晒斑。一个 SPF 等于 15 分钟。
5. 如果你们去游泳或进行其他水上运动，你会暴露在太阳光下很长时间，因此需要用 SPF 超过 30 的防晒品。

图 2-26

图 2-27

Ⅲ. 拓展活动
Ⅲ. Extension Activities

Read typical expressions on Advice and Suggestion, then practice in pairs.

Advice and Suggestion

1. Can I give you some suggestions?
   我能提些建议吗？
2. I'd recommend that you try to relax.
   我建议你放松。
3. What do you think I should do?
   你认为我该怎么做？
4. I suggest you do what he says.
   我建议你按照他说的那样做。
5. What would be your suggestion?
   你的建议是什么？

第三单元 美容前台英语会话
Unit Three Oral English for Beauty Receptionist

任务一 第一次预约
Task One The First Appointment

图 3-1

Ⅰ. 热身活动
Ⅰ. Warm up Activities

A. Learn professional words and expressions.

Common Skin Care Products

foaming cleanser	泡沫式洁面乳
facial milk	洗面奶
facial cleanser	洁面乳
toner	*n.* 爽肤水
mousse	*n.* 摩斯
day cream	日霜
night cream	夜霜
eye cream	眼霜

eye essence 眼部精华

B. Look at these pictures and point out what they are.

图 3-2

图 3-3

图 3-4

图 3-5

Conversation 3.1

图 3-6

The First Appointment of a New Client

Betty—a beauty receptionist　　Eliza—a new client

Betty: Hello, this is Angel Beauty Salon. I'm Betty. Can I help you?

Eliza: Hello, I'm Eliza. Yesterday I received a leaflet of your beauty salon in front of the supermarket. It is said you are having some promotional campaigns because of annual celebration. Is it true?

Betty: Yes, this month we'll have our eighth annual celebration. We are having promotional campaigns to pay back our regular clients' great support during these years, and we also set up some programs for new clients. Would you like to become our new customer?

Eliza: Um... Let me think about it. What are your promotional campaigns?

Betty: You can experience a facial treatment by 50% discount. Our beauty adviser will test and analyze your skin condition for free and give you some advice on how to choose and use skin care products to promote your skin quality. When will you be free to come here?

Eliza: Mm, Maybe tomorrow afternoon. In autumn, my skin is very dry and I want to

图 3-7

know how to keep moisturized.

Betty: No problem. We have some good quality lotion and cream for keeping moisture. There are also some facial treatment programs for keeping moisture in autumn.

Eliza: Oh, I hope so. Bye-bye.

Betty: Wait for a minute, please. Would you tell us your telephone or mobile phone number? I'll call you in advance to remind you tomorrow morning.

Eliza: My mobile phone number is 139××××8490. I'm sure to come tomorrow. See you.

Betty: See you tomorrow.

图 3-8

New Words and Expressions

leaflet[ˈliːflit]　　　　　　　　　　　n. 宣传单
annual[ˈænjuəl]　　　　　　　　　　adj. 每年的，年度的
celebration[ˌseliˈbreiʃən]　　　　　　n. 典礼，庆祝
mobile[ˈməubail]　　　　　　　　　adj. 移动的，活动的

annual celebration	周年庆贺
pay back	回报
favorite activities	优惠活动
mobile phone	手机

图 3-9

Ⅱ. 实践活动
Ⅱ. Practical Activities

A. Practice saying the numbers: please tell us your age, birthday date, zip code, telephone number, room number. What other numbers can you think of?

B. Fill in the blanks.
1. Yesterday I received a _____ of your beauty salon in front of the supermarket.
   昨天我在超市门口收到你们美容院的一份传单。
2. This month we'll have our eighth _____ _____.
   这个月庆祝我们开店8周年。
3. You can experience a _____ _____ by 50% discount.
   你可以半价体验一次面部护理。
4. I want to know how to _____ _____?
   我想知道如何保湿?
5. I'm _____ to come tomorrow.
   我明天一定会来。

C. Translate the following sentences into English.
1. 听说你们因为周年庆有些优惠活动。
2. 我们不仅有一些优惠活动回馈我们老顾客这么多年的支持,也有一些针对新客户的活动。
3. 我们的美容顾问会免费为你测试和分析皮肤状况,并就如何挑选和使用护肤品以提高肤质给你提供一些建议。
4. 我们有一些高品质的保湿乳液和面霜,也有一些专门针对秋季保湿的面部护理项目。

5. 你能给我你的电话或手机号码吗？我明天早上事先打电话提醒你。

Ⅲ．拓展活动
Ⅲ．Extension Activities

Read typical expressions on Talking about Dates and then practice in pairs.

Talking about Dates

1. —What's the date today?
   今天几号？
   —It's September 10th.
   今天 9 月 10 号。

2. School starts on 23rd. We have three days left.
   学校 23 号开学，我们还有三天。

3. —Is the 31st on a Monday?
   31 号是星期一吗？
   —No, it's Tuesday.
   不，是星期二。

4. My birthday is on July 22nd. Please come to my birthday party.
   我的生日是 7 月 22 号，请来参加我的生日聚会。

5. I leave for Shanghai on the 11th of next month.
   我下个月 11 号去上海。

任务二　电话预约和回访
Task Two　Phone Appointment and Post-service Interview

图 3-10

Ⅰ. 热身活动
Ⅰ. Warm up Activities

A. Learn professional words and expressions.

Types of Masks   膜的种类

facial mask	面膜
ice mask	冻膜
seaweed mask	海藻膜
firming mask	紧肤面膜
moisturizing mask	滋润面膜
deep hydration mask	深层补水面膜
neck mask	颈膜
eye mask	眼膜
body mask	体膜
Chinese herb mask	中草药膜

B. Look at these pictures and point out what they are.

图 3-11

图 3-12

图 3-13

图 3-14

图 3-15

Conversation 3.2

A Regular Client's Appointment

Betty—a beauty receptionist   Diana Smith—a regular client

Betty: Hello, this is Angel Beauty Salon. I'm Betty, a beauty receptionist. What can I do for you?

Diana Smith: This is Diana Smith. I want to do facial care at 2:00 this afternoon. Can I ask Alice to do it for me?

Betty: You said you'd like to have facial care at 2:00 pm, right? Let me check the reservation list. Oh, sorry, Alice has an appointment with another client at that time. May I arrange another beautician for you today? How about Anna? She's a new beautician, but…

Diana Smith: Sorry, I don't accept a new comer. Alice is the only one.

图 3-16

Betty: Anna is the champion of provincial cosmetology competition this year. She is very good at massage and acupressure. You sound a bit tired and really need a relaxation. Would you have a try this time?

Diana Smith: Yes, I would. I'm really exhausted.

Betty: OK. We'll wait for your coming at 2:00 pm. See you then.

Diana Smith: See you.

(*The next day, Betty interviews Mrs Smith on the phone.*)

Betty: Hello, This is Betty of Angel Beauty Salon. Is that Mrs Smith?

Diana Smith: It's me.

Betty: How did you feel about Anna's service yesterday?

Diana Smith: It's wonderful. I haven't been so relaxed recently. I had a good sleep that afternoon. Thank you very much.

Betty: You're welcome. Do you remember to have moisturizing masks regularly at home?

Diana Smith: Yes, I do it once every three days. I feel my skin is more moisturized than before.

Betty:Excellent. Will you come at the same time next week?

Diana Smith:Yes,if I'm free.

Betty:All right,I'll send a short message to remind you on Monday.

Diana Smith:Thank you for everything you've done. Good-bye.

Betty:You are welcome. Bye-bye.

图 3-17

New Words and Expressions

appointment[ə'pɔintmənt]　　　　　n. 约会,任命

interview['intəvju:]　　　　　　　n./v. 访谈,面试

arrange[ə'reindʒ]　　　　　　　　vt. 安排,计划

champion['tʃæmpjən]　　　　　　n. 冠军,优胜者

provincial[prə'vinʃəl]　　　　　　adj. 省的,地方的

competition[ˌkɔmpi'tiʃən]　　　　n. 竞争,比赛

exhausted[igˈzɔːstid]　　　　　　adj. 用完的,精疲力竭的

moisturized['mɔistʃəˌraizd]　　　adj. 加水分的,增加湿度的

message['mesidʒ]　　　　　　　n. 消息,信息

remind[ri'maind]　　　　　　　　vt. 使想起,提醒

Ⅱ. 实践活动
Ⅱ. Practical Activities

A. Speak out the following numbers in English.

1. 11　12　20　50　90　100　1000　10000　100000
2. 1975　2008　2010　2050
3. March 21,1987　April 24,1991　May 19,2000
4. 8:00 am　6:30 am　1:20 pm　7:50 pm

B. Read the conversation and then fill in the form.

Client's name	Appointed time	Program	Beautician's name	Receptionist's name	Note

C. Read the dialogue in pairs and then fill in the missing words.

B: Hello, I'm Betty of Angel Beauty Salon. Is it Mrs Smith?

D: It's me.

B: How did you feel Anna's service the day before?

D: 1. _____. I haven't been so relaxed recently. I had a good sleep that afternoon. Thank you very much.

B: 2. _____. Do you remember to have masks to keep moisturized at home?

D: Yes, I do it 3. _____. My skin is more moisturized than before.

B: Excellent. Will you come to our beauty Salon 4. _____ next week?

D: Yes, 5. _____.

B: All right, I'll send you a short message to remind you on Monday.

D: OK. Good-bye.

B: Bye-bye.

D. Translate the following sentences into English.

1. 你好,这里是安琪儿美容院。我是美容前台贝蒂。我能为你做点什么吗?
2. 我是戴安娜·史密斯。我想今天下午两点做一个面部护理,可以要求爱丽丝给我做吗?
3. 对不起,爱丽丝在那个时间已经预约了一位顾客。我今天可以安排其他的美容师为你服务吗?
4. 安娜是今年省美容比赛中的冠军,她很擅长指压和按摩。
5. 我们在下午两点等待你的到来,到时见。

图 3-18

Ⅲ. 拓展活动
Ⅲ. Extension Activities

Read typical expressions on Talking Time and then practice in pairs.

Talking Time

1. —What time is it now?
   现在几点?
   —It's about half past three.
   大约三点半。

2. —What time will you be back?
   你什么时候回来?
   —About a quarter to ten.
   十点差一刻。

3. Our school is over at twenty past four pm.
   我们学校下午四点二十放学。

4. It's time to class/go home.
   该上课了/该回家了。

5. The library starts/opens at nine in the morning.
   图书馆上午九点开门。

第四单元 美容顾问英语会话
Unit Four   Oral English for Beauty Adviser

任务一   到店服务
Task One   Service in the Beauty Salon

图 4-1

Ⅰ. 热身活动
Ⅰ. Warm up Activities

A. Learn professional words and expressions.

Procedures of Admitting Clients

greeting	n. 迎接
counsel	n. 咨询
diagnosis	n. 诊断
plan	n. 计划
implementation	n. 实施
feedback	n. 反馈
assessment	n. 评估

revisit   v. 回访

home treatment guide   家庭护理指导

B. Look at these pictures and point out what they are doing.

图 4-2

图 4-3

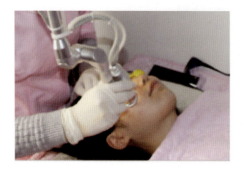

图 4-4

图 4-5

Conversation 4.1

Plan, Evaluation and Feedback

图 4-6

Mary—a beauty adviser   Diana Smith—a client

Mary: Good morning, Mrs Smith. I'm Mary, a beauty adviser of Angel Beauty Salon. Please come in. How are you recently?

Diana Smith: Not very well. I think I need a facial treatment.

Mary: Your complexion is poor and your skin is rather dry. You must be very tired recently. Would you like to have a facial treatment with a seaweed mask? It's good for moisturizing and softening your skin, you will feel refreshed soon.

Diana Smith: OK.

图 4-7

Mary: And you should regularly do eye treatment and eye essence ampoule introduction. Do you have time today?

Diana Smith: Um, How long will they take?

Mary: Two hours together.

Diana Smith: OK. I'll do it now.

(Two hours passed, Mary talked with Diana Smith.)

Mary: Mrs Smith, your complexion looks so nice. Are you satisfied with Anna's service?

Diana Smith: Yes, she's excellent. I want to know how often I should come here.

Mary: You'd better come here once a week for facial treatment. Remember to have water mask every other day at home to keep your skin moisturized. Would you come here at the same time next week?

Diana Smith: Maybe.

Mary: OK. I would call you one day in advance to confirm that.

Diana Smith: You'd better send a short message to me on that day. See you next time.

Mary: Looking forward to seeing you next week.

New Words and Expressions

evaluation [iˌvæljuˈeiʃən]　　　　　　　　　n. 估价,评价

recently [ˈriːsntli]   adv. 最近
complexion [kəmˈplekʃən]   n. 肤色,面色
seaweed [ˈsiːwiːd]   n. 海草,海藻

Ⅱ. 实践活动
Ⅱ. Practical Activities

A. Mark the statements True (T) or False (F).

( ) 1. Mary is a beauty adviser.
( ) 2. Mrs Smith is very well today.
( ) 3. Diana is very tired and wants to have a facial treatment.
( ) 4. Seaweed mask is good for moisturizing the skin.
( ) 5. Facial treatment will take two hours.

B. Fill in the missing words.

1. Your complexion is _____ and your skin is rather _____.
   你的肤色不好而且你的皮肤很干燥。

2. _____ _____ will they take?
   要花多长时间?

3. Mrs Smith, your complexion _____ so nice. Are you _____ with Anna's service?
   史密斯夫人,你的肤色看上去真好,你对安娜的服务满意吗?

4. I want to know _____ _____ I should come here.
   我想知道我多久来一次?

5. You _____ _____ come once a week for facial treatment.
   你最好每周来这儿做一次面部护理。

C. Translate the following sentences into English.

1. 海藻面膜补水效果很好而且能使肌肤柔嫩,你会感觉马上就恢复了精神。
2. 你应该定期做眼部护理和眼部精华导入。

图 4-8

3. 记得每隔一天在家做一次水膜来护理你的皮肤。
4. 你会在下周的相同时间来这儿吗?
5. 我会在头一天打电话去确认。

Ⅲ. 拓展活动
Ⅲ. Extension Activities

Read typical expressions on Delights and Surprises then practice in pairs.

图 4-9

Delights and Surprises

1. This is such a surprise.　　　这真让人惊奇。
2. I can't believe how good it is.　　简直好得让我难以置信。
3. How delightful!　　　　　　　真令人高兴!
4. This is terrific.　　　　　　　太好了!
5. That's fantastic!　　　　　　　太棒了!

任务二　客户交流
Task Two　Communication with Clients

图 4-10

Ⅰ. 热身活动
Ⅰ. Warm up Activities

A. Learn professional words and expressions.

Common Symptoms of Sub-health State

headache	n.	头疼
backache	n.	背疼
fatigue[fə'ti:g]	n.	疲劳
insomnia[in'sɔmniə]	n.	失眠
constipation[ˌkɔnsti'peiʃən]	n.	便秘
dry eyes		眼睛干涩
yellow face		脸色微黄
gray face		脸色灰白

B. Look at these pictures and point out what they are suffering from.

图 4-11

图 4-12

图 4-13

图 4-14

Conversation 4.2

Setting up the Client's Record

Mary—a beauty adviser   Eliza—a client

图 4-15

Mary: Eliza, in order to provide better service, we'll set up a client's record for you. Would you please answer my questions? I'll write them down for you.

Eliza: OK.

Mary: Your full name, please?

Eliza: Eliza Brown.

Mary: Oh, Miss Brown. What is your age and birthday?

Eliza: 25 years old. I was born on Apr. 25th, 1992. Call me Eliza please.

Mary: Ok, Eliza, your telephone or mobile phone number?

Eliza: My mobile number is 137×××related×5986. Remember not to call me at working time, besides, you can send short messages to me at any time.

Mary: I see. Are you single or married?

Eliza: I'm single.

Mary: Well, your registered client number is 298. We'll record all the information about the programs you had here, your timely skin conditions, the products you bought and their prices. Now let's talk about some details. Do you have regular sleeping? When do you usually go to bed at night?

Eliza: I usually sleep at 11:00 pm or later for some extra work.

Mary: In general is your bowel movement normal?

Eliza: Yes, for the most part, but I have a little constipation of late.

Mary: Have you had any illness or physical problems recently?

Eliza: I've had the odd cold as everyone else, sometimes I had a headache, backache and dry eyes while I'm too tired.

Mary: Do you drink or smoke?

Eliza: No. I like coffee, sometimes tea.

Mary: What kind of food do you like?

Eliza: Spicy and sour.

Mary: Do you like sports?

Eliza: I haven't much time to do sports. I just go out for a walk or have yoga at home sometimes.

图 4-16

图 4-17

Mary: That's great. You'd better form good living and eating habits to keep healthy skin. For example, regular exercise, at least three times a week and half an hour every time. Staying up too late is harmful to your skin, you'd better go to bed before 10:00 pm. Having a balanced diet, remember to have light food, drink plenty of water and have more vegetables and fruits every day.

Eliza: Thank you for your advice.

Mary: Don't mention it.

Eliza: Look forward to your coming next time. Goodbye.

Mary: Okay. Bye-bye.

图 4-18

图 4-19

New Words and Expressions

record['rekɔːd]	n. 记录,记载 v. 记录,显示
message['mesidʒ]	n. 消息,信息
single['siŋgl]	adj. 单一的,单个的
married['mærid]	adj. 已婚的,婚姻的
detail['diːteil]	n. 细节,琐事
extra['ekstrə]	adj. 额外的

bowel[ˈbauəl]	n. 肠,内部
odd[ɔd]	adj. 奇数的,古怪的,零散的
spicy[ˈspaisi]	adj. 辛辣的,香的
sour[ˈsauə]	adj. 酸的
yoga[ˈjəugə]	n. 瑜伽
a couple of	两个,几个
balanced diet	均衡饮食
light food	清淡的食物

Ⅱ. 实践活动
Ⅱ. Practical Activities

A. Read the conversation and mark the statements True (T) or False (F).

(   ) 1. Miss Brown is a client.
(   ) 2. Eliza was born on Apr. 20th.
(   ) 3. Eliza doesn't tell her telephone number.
(   ) 4. You can call Eliza at any time.
(   ) 5. Eliza has yoga at home regularly.

B. Read in pairs and fill in the missing words.

1. _____ _____ _____ provide better service, we'll set up a client's record for you.
   为了提供更好的服务,我们将给你建立客户档案。
2. _____ _____ your age and birthday?
   请问你的年龄和生日?
3. _____ _____ _____ call me at working time.
   在我上班的时候记得不要给我打电话。
4. Are you _____ _____ _____?
   你单身还是已婚?
5. Do you have _____ _____?
   你睡觉有规律吗?

C. Translate the following sentences into English.

1. 晚上通常什么时候上床睡觉?
2. 你大便规律吗?
3. 你最近得过什么病或有什么身体问题?
4. 你抽烟或喝酒吗?
5. 你喜欢什么口味的食物?

图 4-20

Ⅲ. 拓展活动
Ⅲ. Extension Activities

Read typical expressions on Invitations then practice in pairs.

Invitations

图 4-21

1. Let's go to the library.
   我们去图书馆吧。
2. Do you want to come to our party? We'd like to see you.
   想参加我们的聚会吗？我们都想见到你。
3. Thanks for your invitation.
   谢谢你的邀请。
4. Are you free tomorrow? Why don't you come over?
   明天你有空吗？为什么不过来呢？
5. Would you like to watch a movie with me?
   你想和我去看电影吗？

任务三 居家护理指导
Task Three   Home Treatment Guide

图 4-22

Ⅰ. 热身活动
Ⅰ. Warm up Activities

A. Learn professional words and expressions.

Common Cosmetics

make-up remover	卸妆产品
foaming cleanser	泡沫式洁面乳
tonic lotion	爽肤水
astringent	n. 紧肤水
essential lotion	精华液
eye cream	眼霜
eye essence	眼部精华
sunscreen lotion or cream	防晒乳液或防晒霜

B. Look at these pictures and point out the order of applying them.

图 4-23

图 4-24

图 4-25

图 4-26

图 4-27

图 4-28

Conversation 4.3

Skin Care at Home

图 4-29

Mary —a beauty counselor   Diana Smith —a client

Mary:Mrs Smith,How nice your complexion looks.

Diana Smith:Really,that's a good news for me.

Mary:How do you have skin care at home? What products do you have?

Diana Smith:After washing my face in warm water with foaming cleanser,I apply some lotion,day cream or night cream.

Mary:Good. If you make up heavily,you'd better choose proper make-up removal lotion to wash your face until it's completely clean.

Diana Smith: Once I make up, I usually clean it thoroughly as soon as I come back home.

Mary: You should use make-up removal to clean your face first even if you don't make up and then clean with foaming cleanser. The next step is to pat some lotion or astringent on your face and neck for replenishing water and moisturizing.

Diana Smith: Do you think I should use any essences?

Mary: Of course, essences and eye cream or eye essence are necessary for people over thirty. They're applied before using day cream or night cream.

Diana Smith: In summer, I use sunscreen products.

Mary: Well, it's a good habit to protect our skin from sunshine every day, not just in summer. In fact, regular exercise and healthy lifestyle are more effective and practical. Any expensive products can't be compared with them.

Diana Smith: I see. Thank you.

Mary: Not at all.

New Words and Expressions

complexion [kəmˈplekʃən]	n. 肤色,面色,体质
pat [pæt]	n./v. 轻拍,轻打
replenish [riˈpleniʃ]	vt./vi. 补充,再装满
essence [ˈesns]	n. 精华,本质

Ⅱ. 实践活动
Ⅱ. Practical Activities

A. Read the conversation and mark the statements True (T) or False (F).

(   ) 1. Mrs Smith cleans her face thoroughly with make-up removal when she has made up.

(   ) 2. You need to clean with make-up removal everyday partly because the air is polluted heavily now.

(   ) 3. Essences are applied after night cream.

(   ) 4. It's necessary to pat some astringent on your neck as well as your face.

(   ) 5. Healthy eating habits are effective for your skin health.

B. Read in pairs and then fill in the missing words.

1. Mrs Smith, _____ _____ your complexion looks.
   史密斯夫人,你今天的脸色真好。

2. Really, that's a _____ _____ _____ me.
   真的啊,对我来说这是好消息。

3. How do you _____ _____ _____ at home?

你在家是怎么做皮肤护理的?

4. In summer, I use _____ _____ _____.
在夏天,我用些防晒产品。

5. It's a good habit to _____ _____ _____ _____ sunshine every day.
每天防晒是个好习惯。

C. Translate the following sentences into English.

1. 如果你化浓妆,你最好选择合适的卸妆液洗脸直到完全清洁。
2. 即使没有化妆,你每天回家也要先用卸妆乳再用泡沫式洗面奶清洗脸部。
3. 对于三十多岁的人来说精华素和眼霜或眼部精华素是必需的,它们都要在日霜或晚霜之前使用。
4. 每天防晒是个好习惯,并不仅仅在夏天。
5. 有规律的锻炼和健康的生活方式更有效、更实用,任何昂贵的产品都不能与之相提并论。

图 4-30

Ⅲ. 拓展活动
Ⅲ. Extension Activities

Read typical expressions on Wishes and Congratulations then practice in pairs.

图 4-31

Wishes and Congratulations

1. I wish you well. Good luck!
   我祝福你。祝你好运!
2. You have my best wishes. I'm sure you'll do fine.
   给你我最好的祝福!我相信你会做得很好。
3. Good job! Please accept my warmest congratulations.
   干得好!请接受我最诚挚的祝贺。
4. That's great! I'm sure you deserve it.
   太好了!我相信这是你应得的。
5. You are outstanding!
   你太棒了!

第五单元　美容师英语会话
Unit Five　Oral English for Beautician

任务一　皮肤的种类和问题
Task One　Types of Skin and Skin Problems

图 5-1

Ⅰ. 热身活动
Ⅰ. Warm up Activities

A. Learn professional words and expressions.

Types of Skin and Problems

dry	*adj.*	干性的
oily	*adj.*	油性的
normal	*adj.*	中性的
mixed	*adj.*	混合性的
sensitive	*adj.*	敏感性的
pimple	*n.*	粉刺,小脓包
acne	*n.*	粉刺,痤疮
rash	*n.*	皮疹
wrinkle	*n.*	皱纹
pore	*n.*	毛孔
blackhead	*n.*	黑头

B. Look at these pictures and point out what skin problems they have.

图 5-2

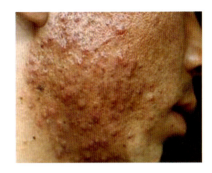
图 5-3

图 5-4

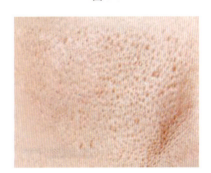
图 5-5

C. Look at these pictures and point out what skin types they are.

图 5-6

图 5-7

图 5-8

图 5-9

图 5-10

Conversation 5.1

Solutions to Different Skin Problems

图 5-11

Mary is a beauty adviser. Ida, Eliza, Grace and Diana Smith are clients. They're having a talk on skin problems. First, Mary assists clients to identify their skin types and then gives them proper advice.

Mary: Hello, I'm Mary, a beauty adviser here. As we know, people have different types of skin. Ida, do you know what types of skin there are?

Ida: There're five types of skin: dry, oily, normal, mixed and sensitive.

Mary: Absolutely right. We can check your skin type with this skin analysis apparatus. Actually, we can also simply know our skin type by observing how much oil your skin produces. Ida, do you know your skin type?

Ida: I'm oily skin. Just as many young boys and girls, I have many pimples and acne on my forehead and nose.

Mary: You're prone to form acne skin and you'd better pay more attention to skin cleansing and choose light lotion or cream. Remember to eat less spicy food. Eliza, how about you?

Eliza: I am prone to have red spots when I try new products or eat seafood, especially little shrimps.

Mary: Obviously, your skin is sensitive. You ought to be cautious to choose and use soft skin care products and eat less seafood.

Grace: I'm Grace, maybe my skin is dry. I pat much toner every day, but my skin is still dry. What should I do?

Mary: You should add oil as well as water so as to keep the balance of water and oil on your skin.

Diana Smith: I also feel my skin is dry and tight.

Mary: Mrs Smith, you are dry on the cheeks while being oily on the T-zone, so you have mixed skin.

图 5-12

Diana Smith: Oh, what should I do?

Mary: It's very important to replenish water and keep moisture at any time, especially for people with dry and mixed skin. It's better to have moisturizing masks daily or at least three times a week.

Diana Smith: Thank you.

Mary: My pleasure.

New Words and Expressions

stimulate['stimjuleit]	vt. 刺激,激励,鼓舞 vi. 起刺激作用
spicy['spaisi]	adj. 辣的
shrimp[ʃrimp]	n. 虾
frown[fraun]	n. 皱眉
cheek[tʃi:k]	n. 面颊
anti-aging['ænti'eidʒiŋ]	n. 抗衰老
analysis[ə'næləsis]	n. 分析,解析
apparatus[ˌæpə'reitəs]	n. 器官,装置,机构,组织,仪器
moisturize['mɔistʃəraiz]	vt. 给……增加水分,使……湿润
skin analysis apparatus	皮肤分析仪

Ⅱ. 实践活动
Ⅱ. Practical Activities

A. Read the conversation and mark the statements True (T) or False (F).

(　) 1. If your skin is dry, you just need to add water every day.

(　) 2. If you have oily skin, you'll have many pimples on your mouth and face.

(　) 3. Don't eat too much seafood if you have sensitive skin.

(　) 4. Be cautious to eat spicy food if you have oily skin.

(　　) 5. It's better to have moisturizing mask every day.

B. Read in pairs and then fill in the blanks of the table.

Name	Skin type	Symptom	Solution
	oily		
Eliza	sensitive		use soft products and eat less seafood
Grace	dry		
Diana Smith		oily on the T-zone, dry on the cheeks	

C. Translate the following sentences into English.
1. 通过观察油脂的分泌情况,我们也能简单地了解皮肤的类型。
2. 我是油性皮肤。正如很多年轻的男孩和女孩一样,在我的额头和鼻子上有很多的小脓包和痤疮。
3. 你是油性皮肤,最好选择清爽的乳液或霜。记得不吃或少吃刺激的食物,如辛辣的食物。
4. 很明显你是敏感性皮肤。你应该谨慎地去选择和使用温和的护肤产品且少吃海产品。
5. 在任何时候,补水和保湿都是很重要的,对于干性或是混合性肌肤的人来说尤其如此,最好每天或是至少一周三次使用保湿面膜。

图 5-13

Ⅲ. 拓展活动
Ⅲ. Extension Activities

A. Read typical expressions on Complaints and then practice in pairs.

Complaints

1. I want to make a complaint.
   我想投诉。
2. I will not stand for this.

图 5-14

我受不了了。

3. This is intolerable.

 这无法容忍。

4. I'm going to complain about it.

 我要对此投诉。

5. I've had it up to here with you.

 我受够你了。

B. Read the passage and then answer the following questions.

Causes and Solution to Acne

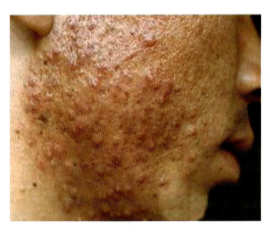

图 5-15

From the moment you are born, your skin begins a lifelong process of shedding dead cells and producing oil. This process can be disrupted by your hormone balance, which changes throughout your life. The acne cycle is initiated when excess oil and dead skin cells combine to plug the pore of a hair follicle; behind the plugged pore, bacteria grow and multiply, triggering inflammation and swelling. That's an acne blemish.

Acne Is Surprisingly Common

People with acne often feel incredibly alone but the fact is, acne is the most common skin disease in the world, with tens of millions of sufferers. More than 85% of Americans have acne breakouts at some time in their lives. Among teenagers, about 90% develop acne, and it can last all their teen years. Many adults have acne, too. Among adult women, about 50% experience acne breakouts at some point; among men, about 25%, and the chronic nature of the condition means adults may have to endure symptoms for decades if not treated.

Choosing an Acne Care System

The vast majority of acne breakouts can be successfully treated with topical over-the-counter medications. However, some more severe cases of inflammatory acne may require a combination of topical and oral medications prescribed by a dermatologist. Prescription treatments are required to be administered under a doctor's care because they have the potential to cause unwanted-and sometimes quite serious-side effects. For mild to moderate acne, regular maintenance therapy with a system that combines topical over-the-counter treatments is the safe and preferred way to go.

1. What are causes of acne?

2. Why is acne the most common skin disease?

3. How do we treat acne?

任务二　面部护理
Task Two　Facial Care

图 5-16

Ⅰ. 热身活动
Ⅰ. Warm up Activities

A. Learn professional words and expressions.

Cleansing Products

facial cleanser /cleansing milk	洗面奶
biological cleanser	去黑头洗面奶
cleanser facial cream/foam	洁面霜/泡沫
eye make-up remover	眼部卸妆产品
exfoliator[iks'fɔːlieitə]	n. 去角质产品
exfoliator /scrub/scrubbing cream	磨砂膏
massage oil/cream	按摩油/霜

B. Look at these objects, read their English labels and then translate into Chinese.

图 5-17

图 5-18

图 5-19

图 5-20

图 5-21

图 5-22

New Words and Expressions

necklace['neklis]	n. 项链
earrings['iəriŋz]	n. 耳环
gown[gaun]	n. 长袍
sprayer['spreiə]	n. 喷雾机
faint[feint]	adj. 微弱的,模糊的
residue['reziˌdjuː]	n. 残渣,剩余物

Conversation 5.2

Process of Facial Care

图 5-23

Mary—a beauty adviser　　Diana Smith—a client　　Anna—a beautician

Mary greets Mrs Smith and arranges Anna to give a facial care for her.

Anna: I'm Anna. This way please, Mrs Smith. Please take off your coat, necklace and earrings and put on this gown. Lie down, please. Wait for a moment. I'll prepare materials and equipment for you.

(*After a moment, Anna comes back.*)

Diana Smith: What's this?

Anna: It's a cosmetic sprayer. It will be helpful to open your facial pore to let the dirt and the waste out and nutrient into the skin.

Diana Smith: Oh, I see. What will you do during facial care?

Anna: First I'll give you a make-up removal and then select a gentle cleansing lotion to clean your face. After the cleansing stage, I'll have an exfoliation with scrubbing cream. Do you know when you had your last exfoliation?

Diana Smith: Last week.

Anna: You really haven't much oil on your face, so we needn't do it this time. But there are some comedones on your nose. Would you allow me to get rid of them? You'll feel a little pain.

Diana Smith: If you do it slightly, I can bear it.

Anna: Believe me, I'll do it carefully. After cleansing and exfoliation, I will massage your face with essential oil for 15~20 minutes and then apply a facial mask. If you have time today, I can give you an eye care.

Diana Smith: How long will they last?

Anna: Two hours together.

Diana Smith: OK. I will do both this time. I would like to have a sleep for a while, so don't talk to me anymore.

图 5-24

Anna: I see. Have a good rest. While cleansing and massaging, please tell me if the pressure is too heavy or light. How are you feeling now, Madam?

Diana Smith: Very comfortable, thank you.

(Two hours later, Anna removed the mask for Mrs Smith.)

Anna: Could you see anything clearly?

Diana Smith: No, I feel a bit faint.

Anna: Well. I will wipe up residue in your eyes. How are you feeling now?

Diana Smith: Much better.

Anna: Now, I have applied some tonic lotion, essence, day cream and sunscreen on your face. They will soon be absorbed. Would you get up or still lie down for a rest?

Diana Smith: Um, I would like to get up and please give me my clothes.

Anna: Here you are.

Diana Smith: Thank you, I really have a good sleep today.

Anna: Wonderful! Please have a glass of water. You look very refreshed now.

Diana Smith: Thank you for your excellent service.

Anna: Don't mention it. Please sign your name at the reception desk. Mary is waiting for you. Remember to come here next week.

Diana Smith: I will, see you next time.

Anna: See you.

Ⅱ. 实践活动
Ⅱ. Practical Activities

A. Read the conversation and mark the statements True (T) or False (F).

( ) 1. You'd better take off your necklace while having facial care.

( ) 2. The beautician clean your face with cleansing foam.

( ) 3. You'd better have an exfoliation every week.

( ) 4. The beautician ought to massage client's face for no more than 20 minutes.

( ) 5. The beautician should ask the client if she can stand the pressure while cleansing and massaging.

B. Read in pairs and fill in the missing words.

1. This way please, Mrs Smith. Please _____ _____ your coat, necklace and earrings and _____ _____ this gown.
   这边请,斯密斯夫人。请脱掉你的外套,项链和耳环且穿上这件长袍。

2. It's a cosmetic sprayer. It will be _____ to open your facial pore to let the dirt and poison _____ and nutrient _____ the skin.
   这是一个美容喷雾机,它有助于打开你面部的毛孔,排出污垢和毒素、吸收营养物。

3. Would you get up or still _____ _____ for a rest?
   你是想起床还是想再睡一下?

4. I can _____ if you do it _____.
   如果轻一点我可以忍受。

5. If you feel _____, I will wipe up _____ in your eyes.
   如果觉得模糊,我会帮你擦去眼睛里的残留物。

C. Translate the following sentences into English.

1. 首先我会为你卸妆,再挑选适合你肌肤的温和的洗面奶清洁面部。
2. 清洁后,我将用磨砂膏去角质。
3. 在清洁和去角质后,我将用精油按摩15～20分钟再敷面膜。
4. 在清洁和按摩时,如果用力太轻或太重请告诉我。
5. 请在前台签名,记得下周来。

图 5-25

Ⅲ. 拓展活动
Ⅲ. Extension Activities

A. Read typical expressions on Plans and Decisions and then practice in pairs.

Plans and Decisions

1. What do you want to do about this mess?

面对这一团糟的状况,你打算怎么做?

2. I haven't made up my mind.
   我还没有下定决心。
3. I plan to take the next train to Nanjing.
   我计划乘坐下一趟火车去南京。
4. The incident was a result of poor planning.
   这次事故是计划不周造成的。
5. I intend to move to Chicago.
   我准备搬到芝加哥去。

B. Read the passage and then answer the following questions.

Practice a Regular Cleansing Routine

图 5-26

　　Cleanse, exfoliate, tone and moisturize-this daily routine should carry you on your way toward healthier skin. Select a gentle skin cleansing solution that works for your specific type of skin-dry, oily or normal. Using your selected product, cleanse face in a circular motion and rinse with lukewarm water, as hot water zaps skin's moisture. Follow the cleansing stage with an exfoliation. The skin of the face is exposed to warm steam, which then opens the pores of the skin. Using a gentle cleanser and other tools, the therapist cleans away the dirt and make-up off of the face. She may also use other tools to slough off blackheads and whiteheads.

　　A granular product is often especially effective in smoothing rough areas and releasing dead skin cells, allowing the face to be better moisturized.

　　After the exfoliation process concludes, use a toner or an astringent to tighten skin and remove any make-up or cleanser residue. A nice alternative to a toner or astringent would be doing a facial mask at least once a week, which tackles clogged pores while also firming skin and leaving it soft and silky.

　　Finally, pat skin dry with a soft towel but do not dry up all the water. Apply a moisturizer (with or without sunscreen) to help protect skin from dryness. Those who have oily skin do not have to moisturize as often as those who have dry, normal or combination skin.

By following the daily skin care routine along with drinking lots of water, exercising and protecting your skin from sun damage, you should soon notice positive results. Maintaining discipline and adhering to your goal to achieve healthier skin make the actual task at hand so much easier to accomplish.

1. Why should we use lukewarm water to clean our face?

1. What is a nice alternative to a toner?

3. What should we do to get healthier skin?

任务三 眼部护理
Task Three Eye Care

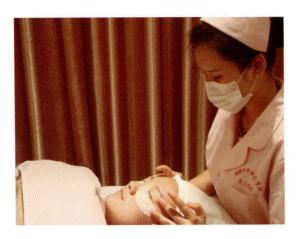

图 5-27

Ⅰ. 热身活动
Ⅰ. Warm up Activities

A. Learn professional words and expressions.

Eye Problems and Solution

dark/black eye circles	黑眼圈
pouches	*n.* 眼袋
puffy eyes	眼睛浮肿

panda eyes　　　　　　　　　　　　　　熊猫眼
eye mask　　　　　　　　　　　　　　　眼贴，眼膜
eye massager　　　　　　　　　　　　　眼部按摩器

B. Look at these pictures and point out what they are doing.

图 5-28

图 5-29

图 5-30

图 5-31

Conversation 5.3

How to Remove Black Eye Circles and Pouches

图 5-32

图 5-33

图 5-34

Mary—a beauty adviser　　　Eliza—a client

Mary: Eliza, let's talk about your skin problems.

Eliza: I'm annoyed about my black eye circles and pouches. Sometimes I feel headache and sore on my neck and back.

Mary: Don't worry. As to black eye circles and pouches, people would have them just because of overworking, too much pressure, staying up too late, drinking too much water after 9:00 pm, or eating too much salty food.

Eliza: Yes, I'm used to staying up late and I can't go to sleep before 12:00 pm because of much work. So I often go to work with panda eyes.

Mary: Too much work and pressure leave people in sub-health state. Over time, not only wrinkles are more visible, our skin tends to lose elasticity and firmness. Therefore, it's essential to use some eye cream and eye essence.

图 5-35

Eliza: Do you have any program to remove black eye circles and pouches?

Mary: We have a new eye care program. Maybe it hasn't obvious improvement within 1~2 months but it really can slow down your aging process, prevent the enlargement of your pouches and relieve your black eye circles.

Eliza: Really, I want to have a try.

Mary: In fact, you can eliminate your black eye circles and pouches if you have enough sleep, drink plenty of water before 9:00 pm and never go to sleep with your make-up on. You can also use some slices of potatoes or apples over the puffy eyes for 10-15 minutes at home to remove puffy eyes.

Eliza: I see. Thank you very much.

Mary: You are welcome.

New Words and Expressions

remove[ri'mu:v]　　　　　　　　　　v. 去除,脱掉

wrinkle['riŋkl]　　　　　　　　　　n. 皱纹 v. 起皱纹

visible['vizəbl]　　　　　　　　　　adj. 看得见的,可见的

elasticity[ˌelæs'tisəti]　　　　　　　n. 弹力,弹性,灵活性

firmness['fə:mnis]　　　　　　　　n. 坚固,坚定

图 5-36

eliminate[i'limineit]　　　　　　　　　v. 消除，去除
sub-health state　　　　　　　　　　　亚健康状态

Ⅱ. 实践活动
Ⅱ. Practical Activities

A. Mark the statements True (T) or False (F).

(　) 1. People have black eye circles and pouches because of too much work and pressure.
(　) 2. People have panda eyes if always staying up too late.
(　) 3. It's essential to use some eye cream and essence for all the people.
(　) 4. You'll have an obvious change in 1-2 months after taking the eye care program.
(　) 5. You can relieve your puffy eyes by applying some banana skin on your eyes.

B. Fill in the missing words.

1. I'm annoyed about my black eye _____ and eye _____.
   我正在为我的黑眼圈和眼袋而烦恼呢。
2. I'm used to _____ _____ _____ and I can't go to sleep before 12:00 pm because of much work.
   我习惯熬夜，由于太多工作，我在晚上十二点之前都不能睡觉。
3. Too much work and pressure leave people in _____ _____.
   太多的工作和压力导致人们处于亚健康状态。
4. You can prevent black eye circles and pouches if you _____ _____ _____.
   如果你能保证充足的睡眠，你可以预防黑眼圈和眼袋。
5. You can also use _____ _____ _____ _____ _____ _____ over the puffy eyes for 10-15 minutes at home to relieve puffy eyes.
   你也可以在家用一些土豆片或苹果片敷在眼睛上10～15分钟来消除肿眼。

C. Translate the following sentences into English.

1. 黑眼圈和眼袋是由于人们加班、压力太大、熬夜、在晚上九点之后喝太多水、吃太咸的食物而产生的。
2. 久而久之，不仅皱纹更明显，我们的皮肤也容易失去弹性和紧实。因此，有必要使用眼霜和眼部精华素。
3. 我们有一个新的眼部护理项目，它真的能延缓你的衰老，阻止眼袋的扩大和减轻黑眼圈。
4. 实际上，如果你能保证充足的睡眠、晚上九点之前多喝水、卸妆后再睡觉，你可以预防黑眼圈和眼袋。
5. 有时我感到头疼而且脖子和后背也疼。

Ⅲ. 拓展活动
Ⅲ. Extension Activities

A. Read typical expressions on Request and Response then practice in pairs.

Request and Response

1. May I see that book?
   我可以看那本书吗？
2. Could I make a small request?
   我可以提一个小要求吗？
3. Why don't you just ask some help at work?
   为什么不要求一下工作上的帮助呢？
4. Could you give me a hand with this heavy box?
   你能帮我搬这个重箱子吗？
5. Would you mind being a little quieter?
   你能安静点吗？

B. Read the passage and then answer the following questions.

Puffy Eye Causes and Solution

图 5-37

Here are some of the most common causes of puffy eyes.

Dehydration

When the body gets dehydrated it begins storing water which can cause puffy eyes.

Diet problems

Consuming alcohol or eating salty foods before going to sleep may cause allergies-your puffy eyes are accompanied by redness or itching.

High blood pressure

High blood pressure pushes fluids into the tissue around the eyes. Puffy eyes can also be caused by diseases like problems with thyroid or kidney infections or simply heredity.

Natural remedies for puffy eyes

There are many methods of preventing or eliminating puffiness. Here are some natural remedies you can try at home.

Keep two teaspoons in the refrigerator and when you have an attack of swollen eyelids, rest them on your eyelids for a minimum of one minute or until they warm up.

Soak cotton pads in a bowl of ice-cold milk and then squeeze most of the liquid out. Place the pad on your eyes and repeat as they warm up for about 15 minutes. They will also brighten the white of the eye.

Soak black or chamomile tea bags in cold water then place them on your eyelids for about 15 minutes. The tannic acid in tea will constrict blood vessels and reduce inflammation.

You can use slices of potatoes or apples over the puffy eyes for 10-15 minutes. Potatoes will reduce dark circles under the eyes and apples have pectin which aids in anti-oxidation.

Puffy eye prevention

You can prevent puffy eyes if you get enough sleep, drink plenty of water in the daytime and never go to sleep with your make-up on.

第六单元　美体师英语会话
Unit Six　Oral English for Body Therapist

任务一　头颈部护理
Task One　Head and Neck Care

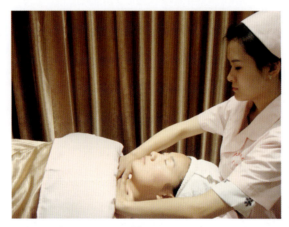

图 6-1

Ⅰ. 热身活动
Ⅰ. Warm up Activities

Learn professional words and expressions.

channels/meridians[məˈridiənz]	n. 经脉
collaterals[kəˈlætərəlz]	n. 络脉
acupoint[ˈækjʊˌpɔint]	n. 腧穴,穴位
acupuncture[ˈækjupʌŋktʃə]	n. 针灸
acupuncturist[ˌækjuˈpʌŋktʃərist]	n. 针灸师
acupressure[ˈækjupreʃə]	n. 指压,指压按摩
massagist[məˈsɑːʒist]	n. 按摩师
urinary[ˈjʊərəˌneri]	adj. 泌尿(器官)的,尿的
bladder[ˈblædə]	n. 膀胱
urinary bladder meridian	膀胱经
channels and collaterals	经络

Conversation 6.1

Head and Neck Massage

图 6-2

Mary—a beauty adviser   Diana Smith—a client

Mary: Mrs Smith, your complexion becomes better and better now.

Diana Smith: Thanks. I keep on wearing moisturizing mask every night. But recently I feel a little uncomfortable in my neck and I don't know why.

Mary: Oh, really? Does it hurt when you turn your head?

Diana Smith: It doesn't hurt actually. I just feel something uneasy with my neck. Definitely it's not "stiff neck", because I never sleep over high pillows.

Mary: I see. You probably have too much office work, or you sit at a desk or a computer for too long.

Diana Smith: That's a bit true. I had loads of business to deal with these days.

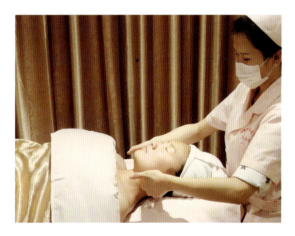

图 6-3

Mary: Another thing is tension. In western medicine, doctors believe tension can narrow your blood vessels, which can cause pain or unpleasantness of your body.

Diana Smith: Wow, you are something of a doctor.

Mary: But traditional Chinese medicine holds that any physical problem comes from the unbalance of "Yin" and "Yang". It is also believed that pain arises when the flow of "Qi" is blocked or slowed down. "Yin", "Yang" and "Qi" are common concepts of traditional Chinese medicine.

Diana Smith: What should I do now?

Mary: In order to promote blood circulation and relieve the pain of head and neck, massage is the best treatment. First, the body therapist will use ice lotion to calm the pain and regulate the injured tissue. You'll feel very cool and comfortable at this stage.

Diana Smith: That's interesting. What will happen next?

Mary: Then she will massage your head and neck with nourishing lotion, which will revitalize your brain cells, and provide new energy and blood for your head and neck.

Diana Smith: Sounds fantastic. I can't wait to have a try.

Mary: And after the massage, you will sleep better and recover from the tension soon. In addition, this massage program can also help to prevent from losing hair. If you would like to have a try now, Anna is available for you at the moment.

Diana Smith: How long will it take?

Mary: About an hour. And you will have a 20% discount if you order 10 times from now on.

Diana Smith: OK. I'll take it into consideration if I feel good.

图 6-4

New Words and Expressions

uneasy [ʌnˈiːzi]	*adj.* 心神不安的,不舒服的	
pillow [ˈpiləʊ]	*n.* 枕头	
tension [ˈtenʃ(ə)n]	*n.* 紧张,不安	*vt.* 使紧张,使不安
vessel [ˈves(ə)l]	*n.* 血管,容器	
balance [ˈbæləns]	*n.* 平衡,均衡,天平	
circulation [ˌsəːkjuˈleiʃən]	*n.* 流通,循环	

regulate[ˈregjuˌleit]	vt. 调整,修复
revitalize[ˌriːˈvaitəlaiz]	vt. 使恢复元气,使新生
available[əˈveiləbl]	adj. 有空的,可获得的
stiff neck	落枕
loads of	大量,许多,一大堆的
have a 20% discount	打八折
take… into consideration	考虑

Ⅱ. 实践活动
Ⅱ. Practical Activities

A. Read the conversation and mark the statements True (T) or False (F).
( ) 1. Mrs Smith looks better because she wears moisturizing masks every night.
( ) 2. Mrs Smith has wrong with her head recently.
( ) 3. Diana had stiff neck before.
( ) 4. Mary has lots of work nowadays.
( ) 5. Diana is in tension so that she feels uncomfortable.

B. Read in pairs and then fill in the missing words.
1. Recently I feel a little _____ in my neck and I don't know why.
   不知道为什么最近我觉得脖子有些不舒服。
2. I just feel _____ _____ with my neck.
   我只是觉得颈部有些不舒服。
3. I had _____ _____ _____ to deal with these days.
   最近我有成堆的事情要处理。
4. You are _____ _____ a doctor.
   你真像个医生。
5. I'll take it into _____ if I feel good.
   如果感觉不错我会考虑的。

C. Translate the following sentences into English.
1. 西医认为压力会导致人体血管变窄,造成身体的疼痛和不适。
2. 传统中医认为任何身体方面的问题都是由于阴阳失衡造成的,疼痛则是因为气不通或不畅。
3. 对于促进血液循环和减轻头颈部的疼痛,按摩是最好的办法。
4. 按摩后,你会睡得更香并且很快就能消除疲劳。此外,它还有助于预防脱发。
5. 如果你现在预订十次,你将享受八折优惠。

Ⅲ. 拓展活动
Ⅲ. Extension Activities

A. Read typical expressions on Certainty and Uncertainty and then practice in pairs.

Certainty and Uncertainty

1. I'm positive that he did it.
   我肯定是他做的。
2. Are you sure this is what you want?
   你确定这是你想要的吗?
3. I have no doubt about how I feel.
   我对我的感觉毫不怀疑。
4. I couldn't say for sure/certain/definite.
   我不确定。
5. I'm not sure if he's telling the truth.
   我不能肯定他是否在说真话。

B. Read the passage and then answer the following questions.

Benefits of Acupressure

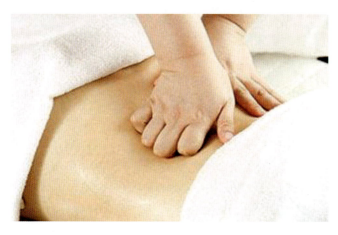

图 6-5

  Acupressure is an ancient healing art that uses the fingers to press key points on the surface of the skin to stimulate the body's natural self-curative abilities. When these points are pressed, they release muscular tension and promote the circulation of blood and the body's life force to aid healing. Acupuncture and acupressure use the same points, but acupuncture employs needles, while acupressure uses the gentle but firm pressure of hands and even feet. There is a massive amount of scientific data that demonstrates why and how acupuncture is effective. But acupressure, the older of the two traditions, was neglected after the Chinese developed more technological methods for stimulating points with needles and electricity. Acupressure, however, continues to be the most effective method for self-treatment of tension-related ailments by using the power and sensitivity of the human hand.

  Foremost among the advantages of acupressure healing touch is that it is safe to do on yourself and others -even if you've never done it before -so long as you follow the instructions and pay attention to the cautions. There are no side effects from drugs, because there are no drugs. And the only equipment needed are your own two hands. You can practice acupressure therapy anytime, anywhere.

1. What is acupressure?

2. What are differences and similarities between acupressure and acupuncture?

3. What are benefits of acupressure?

任务二　背部护理
Task Two　Back Care

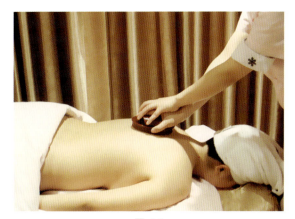

图 6-6

Ⅰ. 热身活动
Ⅰ. Warm up Activities

A. Learn professional words and expressions.

Body Organs　人体器官

heart	n. 心脏
lung [lʌŋ]	n. 肺
belly ['beli]	n. 腹部
stomach ['stʌmək]	n. 胃
bowels ['bauəlz]	n. 肠
liver ['livə]	n. 肝
gallbladder ['gɔːlˌblædə]	n. 胆

kidney['kidni]　　　　　　　　　　　　n. 肾
spleen[spli:n]　　　　　　　　　　　　n. 脾

B. Look at these pictures and point out the equipment for back massage.

1. massage bed　　　2. capricorn brush　　　3. massage oil
4. towels　　　　　　5. pillow

图 6-7

图 6-8

图 6-9

图 6-10

图 6-11

Conversation 6.2

Back Diagnosis and Brush

Mary—a beauty adviser　　　Diana Smith—a client　　　Sally—a body therapist

图 6-12

Mary: Welcome, Mrs Smith. How are you recently?

Diana Smith: My back, neck and shoulders are in pain, maybe because the whole summer I had been staying in the air-conditioning room.

Mary: It's natural for many people to suffer from pain on some parts of their bodies for staying in an air-conditioning room for too long, because the lack of exercising causes the invasion of coldness, the deficiency of "Qi" and poor blood circulation.

Diana Smith: How would you relieve my pain?

Mary: Besides massage, we recommend using five-element essential oil and capricorn brush to brush your body, which can improve blood circulation, eliminate "Qi" stagnation and blood stasis, and make you more energetic and healthier.

图 6-13

Diana Smith: Let me have a look at the brush. Wow, it's so sharp, will it hurt my skin?

Mary: No. Firstly, I will try to brush your back. You'll feel a bit pain, please let me know if you can't stand it.

Diana Smith: Yeah, it really hurts, but I can bear it.

Mary: There are seven reflection areas on a person's back: lung; heart; spleen and stomach; liver and gallbladder; kidney; drainage and reproduction area, which is also called

Baliao Area. Well, now let's have a back diagnosis to find out some physical problems in sub-health state.

Diana Smith: OK.

Mary: After brushing your back, it's obvious to see the clots and nodes on your back. And perhaps you have a headache, dizzy and insomnia sometimes.

Diana Smith: Yes, you're right.

Mary: Your liver and gallbladder area is clearly prominent and there are some obvious black spots, which shows the function of your liver is slowing down. As accumulation of toxins develops, you are likely to have constipation.

Diana Smith: I do have constipation, but not often.

Mary: Your kidney area looks a little dark and your pores are visible, which indicates that you are sensitive to cold weather and your legs and feet are prone to get swollen. All of these problems will arise because of the poor circulation of "Qi" and the blood.

Diana Smith: Wow, it sounds magic.

图 6-14

Mary: Now, Sally is serving you.

Sally: Mrs Smith, I'm very glad to serve you. If you feel intolerable to my brushing or acupressure, please let me know.

Diana Smith: OK. Thank you.

Sally: My pleasure.

(40 *minutes later, Mary gives some advice to Diana Smith after brushing.*)

Mary: Do you still feel pain now?

Diana Smith: No, I'm refreshed and I want to know how long it will take to fade away the redness on my back?

Mary: It depends on your own health. In general it may disappear within one or two hours, but to some weak people, occasionally four or five days.

Diana Smith: Can I have a bath tonight?

Mary: After four hours, the essential oil will be completely absorbed by your skin. So you can have a shower at night. Remember to drink more water or juice.

Diana Smith: Thank you.
Mary: Not at all.

New Words and Expressions

diagnosis [ˌdaiəgˈnəusis]	n. 诊断,判断
invasion [inˈveiʒn]	n. 入侵,侵略
recommend [ˌrekəˈmend]	vt. 推荐,劝告,建议
blockage [ˈblɔkidʒ]	n. 堵塞
node [nəud]	n. 节,瘤,结节
rejuvenate [riˈdʒu:vəneit]	vt. 使……年轻,使……恢复精神
reflection [rɪˈflekʃ(ə)n]	n. 反射,反映
drainage [ˈdreinidʒ]	n. 排水,排泄
reproduction [ˌri:prəˈdʌkʃən]	n. 生殖
clot [klɔt]	n. 凝块,堵塞物
dizzy [ˈdizi]	adj. 头昏眼花的,使人头晕的
insomnia [inˈsɔmniə]	n. 失眠
prominent [ˈprɔminənt]	adj. 显著的,突出的
constipation [ˌkɔnstiˈpeiʃən]	n. 便秘
fade [feid]	vi. 逐渐消逝,失去光泽,褪去
air-conditioning room	空调房

Ⅱ. 实践活动
Ⅱ. Practical Activities

A. Read the conversation and mark the statements True (T) or False (F).

(　) 1. Staying in the air-conditioning room for too long will cause pain in your body.

(　) 2. There're eight reflecting areas on your back.

(　) 3. If your circulation is blocked severely, we'll see some brushed parts become red and purple.

(　) 4. You feel headache, dizzy and insomnia, which shows you have troubles in your neck and back.

(　) 5. There're some black spots on your liver part, which shows the function of your liver is normal.

B. Read in pairs and then fill in the missing words.

1. It's _____ for many people to suffer from pain on some parts of their bodies for _____ in air-conditioning room for too long.

   长时间待在空调房,很多人自然都会感到身体某些部位疼痛。

2. We use capricorn brush and five-element essential oil to brush your back and neck, which can _____ _____ _____.

   我们用摩羯刷和五行精油刷你的背部和颈部,它们能促进血液循环。

3. After brushing your back, it's obvious to see the _____ _____ _____ on your back.
   刷过你的后背之后,在你的后背上看到经络堵塞很明显,还有一些结节。
4. The skin color of your kidney area looks a little dark and your pores are _____, which indicates that you are sensitive to cold weather and your legs and feet are prone to get _____.
   你肾区的肤色看上去有点黑并且你的毛孔很明显,这表明你怕冷且你的下肢容易肿胀。
5. If you feel _____ to my brushing or acupressure, please let me know.
   如果我在刷背和指压按摩的时候,你感到无法忍受,请让我知道。

C. Translate the following sentences into English.

1. 在传统的中医中,认为一个人的背部可以分为七个反射区:肺区,心区,脾胃区,肝胆区,肾区,排泄区和生殖区(也叫八髎区)。
2. 你的肝胆区在后背上有些突出,还有一些黑色斑点,这些黑点表明你的肝脏排毒功能正在下降,导致有毒物质积累。
3. 肾区的肤色看上去有点黑并且你的毛孔很明显,这表明你怕冷且你的下肢容易肿胀。所有这些问题都是由于气血循环不畅引起的。
4. 这取决于你的体质,一般一两个小时就可以消失,但是对于一些体虚的人四五天才能恢复正常。
5. 四小时后,精油就会被皮肤完全吸收。所以你晚上可以洗澡,记住多喝点水或果汁。

图 6-15

Ⅲ. 拓展活动
Ⅲ. Extension Activities

A. Read typical expressions on Belief or Disbelief and then practice in pairs.

Belief or Disbelief

1. I have faith in you.
   我对你有信心。

图 6-16

2. How come you never believe me?
   你为什么总不相信我?
3. I believe that he is trusted.
   我相信他是可信的。
4. I can't believe you've said that.
   我不能相信你竟说出那种话。
5. I'm convinced by his words.
   我被他的话说服了。

B. Read the passage and then answer the following questions.

Back Massage

图 6-17

Required Equipment for Therapeutic Back Massage:
Warm, quiet, relaxed environment.
Firm comfortable surface such as a (firm) bed, massage table or floor mat.
Massage Oil: Baby oil will do fine for a starter.
Towels: To lie on, and also to cover the body.
Cushions or pillows.
Massage Tips:

a. Massage oil decreases the friction created on the skin and prevents the pulling of hairs. Don't use too much. The less oil, the greater the friction and the deeper the pressure.

b. Use slower movements for a soothing or calming response. When applying pressure with finger or thumb, provide support with the other fingers and thumbs. Otherwise you will wear your thumbs out!

c. If the client is uncomfortable in the lower back, ankles, neck or shoulders, place cushions as required under the whole length of the torso, and/or under the ankles, the shoulders, or the side of the head. In pregnancy, the client can lie on her side.

d. Cover any parts of the body not being worked on with a warm towel.

e. Pour the massage oil onto your hands first, and then apply. Once the massage is started, keep a hand on the person at all times, so that there are no surprises.

f. Avoid direct pressure on bony processes. Ask the client for feedback: Are you warm enough? Are you comfortable? How's that feel?

1. What are required equipment for back massage?

2. Why should massage oil be used? What is the effect if using less oil?

3. What can we do if the client feels uncomfortable in the ankles or neck?

4. Why should we keep a hand on the client at all times while starting massage?

5. What should we ask the client while massage?

任务三 水疗法
Task Three SPA

Ⅰ. 热身活动
Ⅰ. Warm up Activities

A. Learn professional words and expressions.

Types of SPA

single essential oil   单方精油

图 6-18

compound essential oil	复方精油
base essential oil	基础油
lymph circulation [limf ˌsəːkjuˈleiʃən]	淋巴引流
sauna [ˈsaunə]	n. 桑拿浴
hydrotherapy [ˈhaidrəuˈθerəpi]	n. 水疗法
mineral mud bath	矿泥浴
hot spring	温泉
hot stone therapy	热石浴
peat pulp bath	泥浆浴
steam bath	蒸汽浴
Vichy [ˈviːʃiː] bath	维希浴
Finnish [ˈfiniʃ] bath	芬兰浴
Turkish bath	土耳其浴

B. Surf online and point out what forms of SPA are in the following pictures.

图 6-19

图 6-20

图 6-21

图 6-22

图 6-23

图 6-24

Conversation 6.3

In the SPA

图 6-25

Betty—a beauty receptionist　　Diana Smith—a client　　Mary—a beauty adviser

Betty: Hello, Mrs Smith. I'm Betty of Angel Beauty Salon. August 8th is the anniversary celebration day of Angel Beauty Salon. Clients who come regularly will be given some preferential treatment, including a ￥100 voucher, a free SPA experience and some other favorable activities. Do you have time to come?

Diana Smith: I'll come this afternoon.

Betty: Great! We'll be waiting for your coming.

(*In the afternoon, Diana is coming.*)

Mary: Welcome, Mrs Smith. Do you know we offer some favorable activities to regular clients this week because of the anniversary?

Diana Smith: Congratulations! Betty has called me this morning. By the way, what is SPA? I know it's water therapy. Does it mean taking a bath or a sauna, or anything else?

图 6-26

Mary: SPA originated from the Latin word *Solus Por Aqua*. *Solus* means health, *Por* means via and *Aqua* means water. SPA is a kind of hydrotherapy that releases pressure and relax body through massage, with cosmetics applied to the body. You will be able to temporarily escape from busy life in a professional SPA beauty center because of its comfortable atmosphere and satisfactory services.

Diana Smith: What services does it include?

Mary: SPA includes massage treatment, acupressure, lymph circulation treatment, facial treatment, body care, aromatherapy, hydrotherapy, mineral mud bath, manicure, etc. As for the facilities, there are sauna room, steam room, nutrition and weight consultation center, diet bar, exercise section, etc. Why don't you have a professional SPA trip this afternoon?

Diana Smith: Terrific!

图 6-27

图 6-28

Mary: You can put your clothes in the lockers before you go into the public pool. You ought to rinse your body thoroughly and wear swim cap so that the water won't be polluted.

Diana Smith: I see. Can you show me where the locker room is?

Mary: This way, please. Just follow me.

Diana Smith: Look! Are they saunas and steam rooms?

Mary: Yes. The temperature in the steam room will be very high. If you feel uncomfortable you must go out at once. Remember not to stay in the water for too long and not to keep the water exceed your heart level while you soak in the hot spring.

Diana Smith: I feel so relaxed in such comfortable environment. By the way, I have bought a wooden barrel in my home. Can I invite a body therapist to instruct me to have a SPA at home?

Mary: Of course! If you want this kind of service, then you just need to call Betty and make an appointment to decide time and the body therapist in advance.

Diana Smith: OK, I see. Thank you.

Mary: You are welcome.

图 6-29

图 6-30

New Words and Expressions

anniversary [ˌæniˈvəːsəri]	n. 周年纪念,周年纪念日
celebration [ˌseliˈbreiʃ(ə)n]	n. 庆祝,庆典
preferential [ˌprefəˈrenʃ(ə)l]	adj. 优惠的,优先的
voucher [ˈvautʃə]	n. 代金券,证人,证据
congratulation [kənˌgrætjuˈleiʃən]	n. 祝贺,恭喜
originate [əˈridʒineit]	vt. 发起 vi. 开始,起源于
Latin [lætin]	n. 拉丁语,拉丁语系国家的人 adj. 拉丁语的
wrap [ræp]	v. 包,裹 n. 围巾,披肩,包装材料
temporarily [ˈtempərərili]	adv. 暂时地,临时地
escape [iˈskeip]	v. 逃避,逃脱
terrific [təˈrifik]	adj. 极度的,极好的

rinse[rins]　　　　　　　　　　　vt. 清洗，冲洗　n. 清洗
locker['lɔkə]　　　　　　　　　　n. 更衣箱，储物柜
exceed[ik'si:d]　　　　　　　　　vt. 超过，超出　vi. 领先
soak[səuk]　　　　　　　　　　　vt. 使浸透，浸洗　vi. 浸泡，渗入
barrel['bærəl]　　　　　　　　　n. 桶，圆筒，桶状物
regular client　　　　　　　　　老顾客，定期到店的顾客

Ⅱ. 实践活动
Ⅱ. Practical Activities

A. Read the conversation and mark the statements True (T) or False (F).

(　) 1. August 8th is the anniversary day of Angel Beauty Salon.
(　) 2. Mrs Smith will come tomorrow afternoon to experience a free SPA.
(　) 3. Sauna is a kind of SPA.
(　) 4. You'd better wear a swim cap so that your hair doesn't get wet.
(　) 5. You can stay in the water as long as you like while soaking in the hot spring.

图 6-31

B. Read in pairs and then fill in the missing words.

1. SPA originated from the Latin word *Solus Por Aqua*. *Solus* means _____, *Por* means _____ and *Aqua* means _____.
   SPA 起源于拉丁文 *Solus Por Aqua*。*Solus* 的意思是健康，*Por* 的意思是通过，*Aqua* 的意思是水。

2. As for the facilities, there are _____ _____, _____ _____, nutrition and weight consultation center, diet bar, exercise section, etc.
   至于设施，有桑拿室、蒸汽室、营养和体重咨询中心、节食吧、健身部等。

3. You can put your clothes in the _____ before you go into the _____ _____.
   进入公共浴池之前你可以把你的衣服放在储物柜。

4. The temperature in the steam room will be very high. If you feel _____ you must go out at once.

   蒸汽室的温度是很高的。如果你感到不舒服，应该马上出来。

5. Can you show me where the _____ _____ is?

   你能告诉我更衣室在哪吗？

C. Translate the following sentences into English.

1. 在一个专业的 SPA 美容中心，由于它舒服的氛围和令人满意的服务，你将能暂时地从繁忙的生活中得到解脱。
2. SPA 包括按摩疗法、指压按摩、淋巴引流、面部护理、身体护理、芳香疗法、水疗法、矿泥浴和美甲等。
3. 你应该彻底地冲洗你的身体且戴上泳帽以保证水不被污染。
4. 在泡温泉的时候不要在水里待太久或是让水漫过心脏。
5. 如果你想邀请一位美体师去家里指导做 SPA，只需要给贝蒂打电话，提前确定时间和美体师就行了。

图 6-32

图 6-33

Ⅲ. 拓展活动
Ⅲ. Extension Activities

A. Read typical expressions on Compliments and Praises and then practice in pairs.

Compliments and Praises

1. You did a good job.

   你干得很好。

2. You have excellent manners.

   你很有风度。

3. You're the best in the business.

   你是这行业里最棒的。

4. I salute your efforts.

   我对你的努力表示钦佩。

5. You look good in red.

   你穿红色很好看。

B. Read the passage and then answer the following questions.

SPA Treatment

图 6-34

SPA originated from the Latin word *Solus Por Aqua*. SPA is a kind of hydrotherapy that releases pressure and lets the body relax through massage, wrapping and applying cosmetics to the body. The body treatment, spa treatment, or cosmetic treatment are non-medical procedures to help the health of the body. It is often performed at a resort, destination spa, day spa, beauty salon or school. Typical treatments include:

- facials—facial cleansing with a variety of products
- massage
- waxing—the removal of body hair with hot wax
- body wraps—wrapping the body in hot linens, plastic sheets and blankets, or mud wraps, often in combination with herbal compounds
- aromatherapy
- skin exfoliation—including chemical peels and microdermabrasion
- nail care such as manicures and pedicures
- bathing or soaking in any of the following:

    hot spring

    onsen (Japanese hot springs)

    thermae (Roman hot springs)

    hot tub

    mud bath

    peat pulp bath

    sauna

    steam bath

- nutrition and weight guidance
- personal training
- yoga and meditation

Recent trends

In recent past, SPA in the US emphasized dietary, exercise, or recreational programs more than traditional bathing activities. Up until recently, the public bathing industry in the US remained stagnant. Nevertheless, in Europe, therapeutic baths have always been very popular, and remain so today. The same is true in Japan, where the traditional hot springs baths, known as onsen, always attracted plenty of visitors. But also in the US, with the increasing focus on health and wellness, such treatments are again becoming popular.

1. What is SPA?

2. What typical SPA treatment can you list?

3. Compare the trend and popularity of SPA in the US, Europe and Japan.

C. Read the passage and then answer the following questions.

Process of SPA

图 6-35

Body SPA therapy is various according to different countries and clients' requirements. But the main processes are as following.

1. Exfoliation

It makes the skin smoother and softer then easier to take in nutrients. The client has a bath or sauna in advance. Spa therapist applies exfoliating products on such parts as back, elbow, knee and feet then use dry towel gourd (sponge, towel or hand) to scrub and get rid of dead skin. Sometimes, dead skin of the feet is so thick that we have to use tougher products such as sea salt or some other assistant tools such as brushes to remove it.

2. Hydrotherapy

It is usually in the water or hot spring with some additions, which can promote blood circulation and make muscles and nerves relaxing. There are various forms such as Vichy, Finnish, Turkey, etc. Some herbs, flowers, milk, essential oil with different effects are added in the water. Now, take flower hydrotherapy as an example.

(1) Prepare clean water with proper temperature and fresh rose flowers in a big wooden barrel or bath tub.

(2) Light scented lamp or candles, turn on light music and create comfortable and relaxing environment.

(3) Lead the client into the water and set up the soaking time according to the client's physical condition, usually no more than 20 minutes. The body therapist has to accompany the client during soaking lest some accident would happen.

3. Body dressing

(1) Dress the body with herb (seaweed, mud or honey, etc.) then pack the body with preservative film or thick bath towel.

(2) Increase body temperature with apparatus such as far infrared space cabin or electric blanket, etc., which is helpful to open the pores and take in the nutrients in the herb dressing.

4. Massage

Use different massage techniques and essential oil to massage different parts of body to achieve the effects of relaxing, promoting circulation and keeping fit. The most popular technique is body lymph circulation.

1. While exfoliating, what parts should be scrubbed with tougher tools?

2. Why is soaking time in the water no more than 20 minutes?

3. What apparatus are used after body dressing and for what reasons?

第七单元 化妆师和美甲师英语会话
Unit Seven　Oral English for Cosmetician and Manicurist

任务一　日妆
Task One　Daily Make-up

图 7-1

Ⅰ．热身活动
Ⅰ．Warm up Activities

A．Learn professional words and expressions.

Common Cosmetic Products

foundation	*n.* 粉底
block base cream	隔离霜
concealer	*n.* 遮瑕霜
loose powder	散粉
pressed powder	粉饼
eye shadow	眼影
mascara	*n.* 睫毛膏
blush compact	腮红

lipstick   n. 口红

B. Identify the following cosmetic accessories and give their English names.

1. eyebrow knife   2. artificial eyelash   3. powder puff
4. eyelash curler   5. blush brush   6. pressed powder

图 7-2

图 7-3

图 7-4

图 7-5

图 7-6

图 7-7

Conversation 7.1

Process of Daily Make-up

图 7-8

Amy—a client   Betty—a cosmetician
Amy: Betty, you look pretty well!
Betty: Thank you. You look good too. No matter where I go, I wear make-ups. You

know make-up is really amazing. It can embellish your complexion and facial features. It can make you look even more beautiful.

Amy: Yeah, as the saying goes, "Nobody is not in love with beauty". Maybe you will feel better after finishing your make-up, but some people treat their faces as plates and put on all kinds of colors. I think that's terrible.

Betty: That's probably due to their lacking of professional knowledge. In fact real make-up is to enhance natural beauty. Therefore the best natural make-up should be as if there's no make-up. It is also called nude make-up.

Amy: Right, but how to get that natural effect?

Betty: First, you should always do basic skin care so that your skin won't be hurt. After that, you can use concealer and foundation to conceal facial defects, improving the look of your skin and even modify your facial features. No matter the shape of your face is square, round or triangle, proper foundation will make you look good.

Amy: Oh! That's why you look so great.

Betty: Right.

Amy: It is said that UV protector is divided into purple and green UV protector. What color UV protector should I choose?

Betty: Your complexion is yellow and gloomy. I think purple UV protector will suit you and make your skin whiter. Green UV protector is suitable to the skin in red.

Amy: After that, what else should I do?

Betty: After the make-up base, you should prune your eyebrows and pencil the eyebrows. Your eyebrows are dense, but they have not three-dimensional effect because of odd hairs. And since your hair is black, you can extend the end of your eyebrow with black eyebrow powder and make it have more three-dimensional effect.

Amy: Yes I am all ears.

Betty: There follows the part of eye make-up. Firstly wear eye shadows in three similar colors and then wear eye liner and mascara. Your eyelashes are a bit long, but not very thick and curly, so I suggest you curl your eyelashes, and then use L'Oreal Paris double extension mascara to make your eyes bigger and more beautiful.

Amy: Have I finished my daily make-up after these processes?

Betty: No, after the eye make-up, you can apply blush compact and lipstick which can embellish your complexion and facial features.

Amy: Wow! It sounds like a lot of fun. Are these all your secrets to your perfect make-up?

Betty: Well, the most crucial and final work is to remove your final make-up thoroughly. That's the secret to permanently possess the magical effects of make-up.

Amy: I see. Thank you very much!

Betty: You are welcome.

New Words and Expressions

magical ['mædʒikəl]   adj. 魔术的,有魔力的,神奇的

图 7-9

embellish[im'beliʃ]	v. 美化,装饰,修饰
enhance[in'haːns]	vt. 提高,增加,加强
defect['diːfekt]	n. 瑕疵,毛病
modify['mɔdifai]	v. 修饰,修改
triangle['traiæŋgl]	n. 三角形
skinny['skini]	adj. 瘦的,皮包骨的
gloomy['gluːmi]	adj. 黯淡的,阴暗的
vigorous['vigərəs]	adj. 精力充沛的
crucial['kruːʃəl]	adj. 关键的,决定性的
permanently['pəːmənəntli]	adv. 永久地

Ⅱ. 实践活动
Ⅱ. Practical Activities

A. Read the conversation and mark the statements True (T) or False (F).

( ) 1. If you want to look nice, you should put all kinds of color on your face.
( ) 2. The best make-up should look natural as if there's no make-up.
( ) 3. You'd better do some skin care before make-up so that you'll look nice.
( ) 4. If your face is square, you'll look terrible after making up.
( ) 5. The secret of successful make-up is to remove your make-up thoroughly before sleeping.

B. Read in pairs and then fill in the missing words.

1. Some people _____ their faces _____ plates and put on all kinds of colors.
   很多人把他们的脸当作色彩盘,在上面画上各种各样的色彩。
2. That's probably _____ _____ their lacks of professional make-up knowledge.
   那可能是因为他们缺乏专业的化妆知识。
3. Before make-up, you should always do basic skin care so that your skin is not

_____.
化妆之前,你应该经常做基础的皮肤护理,这样你的皮肤就不易受到伤害。

4. Green UV protector is well _____ to the skin in red.
   绿色隔离霜非常适合泛红的皮肤。

5. Are these all your _____ to your perfect make-up?
   这些都是你成功化妆的秘诀吗?

C. Translate the following sentences into English.

1. 化妆是神奇的,它能修饰你的肤色和面部容貌。
2. 事实上真正的化妆会增强自然的美感。因此最好的化妆效果应该看上去非常自然,就像没化妆一样。
3. 你可以用遮瑕霜、底妆和粉底去掩盖面部的缺陷,提亮肌肤,修饰面容。
4. 底妆之后,你再上粉、眼影、睫毛膏、眼线液、假睫毛、腮红、口红等。
5. 最关键和最后的工作是彻底地卸妆,那就是永久地拥有神奇的化妆效果的秘诀。

图 7-10

Ⅲ. 拓展活动
Ⅲ. Extension Activities

Read typical expressions on Reassurances and Consolations and then practice in pairs.

Reassurances and Consolations

1. Don't worry about it.
   别担心。
2. Just keep trying.
   加油,别气馁。
3. Things will get better.
   事情会好转的。
4. We all have bad days sometimes.
   我们都会有不顺利的时候。

图 7-11

5. I know how you feel.
   我知道你的感受。

任务二　新娘妆
Task Two　Bridal Make-up

图 7-12

Ⅰ. 热身活动
Ⅰ. Warm up Activities

A. Learn professional words and expressions.

Common Cosmetic Accessories

powder puff　　　　　　　　　　　　粉扑

sponge		n. 海绵
eyebrow knife		眉刀
eyebrow brush		眉刷
eye shadow brush		眼影刷
artificial eyelash		假睫毛
eyelash brush		睫毛刷
eyelash curler		卷睫毛夹
blush brush		腮红刷
lipstick brush		唇刷

B. Match the cosmetics and related accessories

	Cosmetics		Cosmetic accessories
1	foundation	A	eyeliner brush
2	blush compact	B	large eye shadow brush
3	eyeliner	C	powder puff
4	eye shadow	D	eye brow knife
5	lipstick	E	blush brush
6	translucent face powder	F	eyelash curler/mascara
7	eyelash	G	powder puff
8	eyebrow	H	lip brush
9	conceal defect cream	I	eyebrow brush
10	eyebrow	J	embellish brush

Conversation 7.2

Tips of Bridal Make-up

Mary—a beauty receptionist   Helen—a client   Jimmy—a cosmetician

Mary: Good afternoon, what can I do for you?

Helen: I'm getting married. Can you arrange an experienced make-up artist for me?

Mary: Sure. This is Jimmy, our best cosmetician. This is Helen, she wants to make a bridal make-up.

Jimmy: Hello, Helen.

Helen: Hello, Jimmy. Can you help me?

Jimmy: Of course, on the wedding day the bride should be the most beautiful lady and I'm sure to make you the shinning focus on that day.

Helen: Really?

Jimmy: Believe me. Since you need a heavy and beautiful make-up, we should use cosmetics that can keep a long time so that you will look best in photography. Firstly, let me

图 7-13

see your facial features and your skin type. I'll choose proper make-up for you.

 Helen:OK.

 Jimmy:Well,you have a round face and a mixed skin. The T part is oily and the cheek is a bit dry. All right,let me clean your skin first.

 Helen:Thank you. Mm,what did you spray just now?

图 7-14

 Jimmy:I just sprayed silk whitening lotion and smeared nourishing cream,and then I will prune your eyebrows. Your eyebrows are dense,but they have not three-dimensional effect because of the strays. Please raise your head. OK,thanks. I will smear block base cream before I make up.

 Helen:Why should I smear block base cream?

 Jimmy:Because cosmetics will hurt our skin. What kind of wedding dress will you choose?

 Helen:I'd like to choose an open neckline wedding dress.

Jimmy: Well, if your dress has an open neckline, I will sweep your neck and chest with a thin layer of bronzing powder to make them appearing a warm color. I'll give you some tips: carry a touch-up kit with concealer, powder, lipstick or transparent lipstick, lip line pencil and tissue paper. Also prepare a mini sewing kit for sewing clothes in case of emergency. They will be helpful. All right, your bridal make-up is finished.

Helen: Great! Thanks a lot.

Jimmy: My pleasure.

图 7-15

New Words and Expressions

bride[braid]	n.	新娘
wedding['wediŋ]	n.	婚礼, 结婚
focus['fəukəs]	n.	焦点, 中心 v. 聚焦, 调整
spray[sprei]	v.	喷, 喷射 n. 喷雾, 喷雾器
smear[smiə(r)]	v.	涂抹, 敷
neckline['nek‚lain]	n.	领口
tissue['tiʃu]	n.	纸巾
sewing['səuiŋ]	n.	缝纫, 缝制物
kit[kit]	n.	成套工具, 工具箱
emergency[i'mə:dʒənsi]	n.	突发事件, 紧急状态
touch-up kit		补妆包
sewing kit		针线包

Ⅱ. 实践活动
Ⅱ. Practical Activities

A. Read the conversation and mark the statements True (T) or False (F).

( ) 1. Helen wants the receptionist to do bridal make-up for her.
( ) 2. Jimmy is an experienced make-up artist.
( ) 3. Helen's eyebrows aren't very nice because of the strays.
( ) 4. Helen's skin is oily so she needs to smear block base cream.
( ) 5. Jimmy suggests Helen to carry a touch up kit and a sewing kit.

B. Fill in the missing words.

1. Can you arrange an _____ _____ _____ to make my bridal make-up?
   你能安排一个有经验的化妆师给我化新娘妆吗?
2. On the wedding day the bride should be the most beautiful lady and I'm sure to make you _____ _____ _____ on that day.
   在婚礼那天,新娘子应该是最漂亮的女士,我确信能使你成为那天闪亮的焦点。
3. Since you need a heavy and beautiful make-up, we should use _____ that can keep a long time so that you will look best in photography.
   因为你需要浓烈而漂亮的妆容,所以我们要用不掉妆的化妆品而且让你在摄影中看上去是最美的。
4. You have a _____ face and a mixed skin. The T part is _____ and the cheek is a bit dry.
   你的脸型是圆脸,你的皮肤是混合型,T部位有点油,两颊有点干。
5. I'd like to choose an open neckline _____ _____.
   我想选择一件敞开领口的结婚礼服。

图 7-16

C. Translate the following sentences into English.

1. 首先,让我看看你的面部特征和皮肤类型,我将为你选择合适的妆容。
2. 让我先给你清洁皮肤吧,给你清洁皮肤后喷了蚕丝凝白柔肤水,抹了营养霜,接下来给你修眉毛。

3. 你的眉毛挺浓密的,但是因为有些杂毛显得立体感不强。
4. 如果你的礼服有一个敞开的领口,我将在你的脖子和胸部扫上一层薄薄的古铜色散粉,使它们呈现出暖色调。
5. 我给你些小建议:携带一个装有遮瑕膏、粉饼、口红或透明唇膏、唇笔和面纸的补妆包。

Ⅲ. 拓展活动
Ⅲ. Extension Activities

A. Read typical expressions on Warnings and Prohibitions and then practice in pairs.

Warnings and Prohibitions

图 7-17

1. No smoking.
   禁止吸烟。
2. No unauthorized entry.
   禁止入内。
3. No pets allowed.
   宠物禁止入内。
4. Do not enter.
   不得入内。
5. Do not walk on the grass.
   请勿践踏草坪。

B. Read the passage and then answer the following questions.

Make-up and Styling

Make-up and styling are products of an affluent and civilized society. Women can show their beauty, personal style and confidence through proper make-up and styling. As far as facial make-up is concerned, it is important to cover up imperfection, to embellish one's appearance, and to create a three-dimensional effect, sense of beauty and natural feeling.

图 7-18

Make-up and styling is an art and it needs to be handled just as professionally as making perms and dying hair. One must understand color, light, cosmetics characteristics as well as facial characteristics (advantages and disadvantages based on shape and skin quality) in order to be able to choose proper color and product and to do the best make-up and styling. The following are several categories of make-up and styling according to varied needs.

a. General make-up and styling: suitable for indoor and outdoor daily life, visiting, shopping, etc.

b. Banquet make-up and styling: suitable for occasions such as indoor, outdoor, daytime and evening banquets, etc.

c. Wedding make-up and styling: including make-up and styling for the groom, bride, groomsman, bridesmaid and flower boy and girl.

d. Stage make-up and styling: treatment differs depending on required stage effects.

e. Photography make-up and styling: treatment differs depending on required photographic effects.

f. Visionary make-up and styling: including body painting, special effect, and creative make-up and styling.

1. Why women are willing to have make-up and styling?

2. What knowledge should be known as a professional make-up artist?

3. Can you list several kinds of make-up and styling?

任务三 美甲
Task Three Manicure

图 7-19

Ⅰ. 热身活动
Ⅰ. Warm up Activities

A. Learn professional words and expressions.

Manicure Tools

nail polish	指甲油
nail clipper[ˈklipə]	指甲钳
nail file[fail]	指甲锉
nail scissors[ˈsizəz]	指甲剪
nail brush	指甲刷

B. Identify the following manicure tools and give their English names.

图 7-20

图 7-21

Conversation 7.3

Process of Manicure

图 7-22

Helen—a client   Jenny—a manicurist

Helen: Hello, I want to have a manicure.

Jenny: OK, I'm a manicurist, my name's Jenny. Nice to meet you.

Helen: I'm Helen. Nice to meet you, too.

Jenny: Let me trim your fingernails first. OK?

Helen: It looks very nice.

Jenny: Would you like your fingers to look a bit longer than they actually are?

Helen: Of course.

Jenny: I will paste some special transparent plastic pieces on your fingernails.

Helen: All right.

Jenny: Which shape do you prefer? Oval or rectangle?

图 7-23

Helen: Rectangle. I would also like some nail polish.

Jenny: No problem. I think pink is perfect for you.

Helen: OK.

Jenny: There are different kinds of shining powder you can choose. They are gold powder, silver powder, artificial diamond, plastic bows and so on. What kind of powder do you want me to sprinkle on your fake fingernails?

图 7-24

Helen: I feel strange If you paste artificial diamond and plastic bow on my fake fingernails. I prefer the silver powder.

Jenny: All right. Your manicure has been done. It is a very important step to dry your fingernails, otherwise it will spoil its effect. Please put your hands under the manicure drier.

Helen: So professional.

Jenny: The fingernails have been dry, but don't touch your fingernails with sharp and hard things. You should put your hands into cold water about ten minutes after you return home.

Helen: Thank you very much.

Jenny: You are welcome.

New Words and Expressions

trim[trim]	v. 修剪
fingernail[ˈfiŋɡəneil]	n. 手指甲
manicure[ˈmæniˌkjuə]	n. 修指甲，修指甲的人
plastic[ˈplæstik]	n. 塑料，塑料制品
bow[baʊ]	n. 蝴蝶结
sprinkle[ˈspriŋkl]	v. 洒，撒 n. 屑状物
paste[peist]	n. 面团，浆糊 vt. 粘贴

图 7-25

Ⅱ. 实践活动
Ⅱ. Practical Activities

A. Read the conversation and mark the statements True (T) or False (F).

(   ) 1. Jenny is a manicure who can repair and beautify nails for clients.

(   ) 2. Helen likes pink so she asks Jenny to polish pink nail oil for her.

(   ) 3. Jenny can make Helen's fingers seem longer by some special plastic pieces.

(   ) 4. It's the last step to dry fingers under the manicure drier.

(   ) 5. You can touch any hard things with your polished fingernails without any hurt.

B. Read the conversation and then fill in the missing words.

1. Let me _____ _____ _____ first.
   让我先给你修下指甲吧。

2. I would like you to put on some _____ _____.
   我想让你给我涂些指甲油。

3. What kind of powder do you want me to _____ _____ your fake fingernails?
   你想让我撒些什么在你的手指甲上呢?

4. Please put your hands under the _____ _____.
   请把你的双手放在美甲烘干机下。

5. The fingernails have been dry, but don't touch your fingernails with _____ and _____ things.
   指甲已经干了,但是你不要拿一些尖锐的或是硬的东西去碰你的手指甲。

图 7-26

C. Translate the following sentences into English.

1. 我认为粉红色的指甲油很适合你。
2. 我们可以贴些特殊的透明塑料片在你的手指甲上,让指甲显得长一些。
3. 接下来我会撒些金粉、银粉或者贴些假钻石、塑料蝴蝶结等在你的假手指甲上。
4. 你的美甲已经做好了,把双手放在烘干机下烘干是很重要的一步,否则将会影响美甲的效果。

5. 当你回到家的时候，你应该把你的双手放在冷水里泡个 10 分钟左右。

图 7-27

Ⅲ. 拓展活动
Ⅲ. Extension Activities

A. Read typical expressions on Talking about People and then practice in pairs.

Talking about People

1. He is very unusual.
   他非常不同寻常。
2. My coworker is too loud.
   我的同事嗓门太大了。
3. John is the best player we have.
   约翰是我们最好的队员。
4. His parents are very strict on him.
   他的父母对他要求很严格。
5. My brother is always in trouble at school.
   我弟弟在学校总闯祸。

B. Read the passage and then answer the following questions.

Nail Care Tips-Beautiful Nature Nails

Beautiful, natural nails require care and proper manicuring. A short nail that is straight across the top with rounded edges is the current in style shape. Here are nail care tips for polishing your nails so they will look beautiful and stay looking fresh longer.

Filing Nails

File nails when the white part of the nail tip has grown 1/4 from the pink part of the

图 7-28

nail. Filing nails before the nail is 1/4 long can weaken the nail. Allowing the nail to grow to a length longer than the base pink nail length will be sure to make them break easily. Nail files from side to side would weaken nails. When filing, go from the corner to the center in one direction. Follow the groove on the side of your nail.

Buffing Nails

Buffing nails can give them a shinier finish. Start at the cuticle and work your way down to the tip with medium pressure. Don't use a back and forth movement as heat builds up and this can damage your nails. Continue lightly until all ridges on the nail surface have disappeared.

Clean Nails

Be sure that nails are clean and dry, free of any oil or lotion, before applying polish. Remove any old polish from nails.

Base Coat

Always use a base coat and let it dry for at least 1 minute. The base coat helps to keep nail polish from chipping and makes polish last longer.

Applying Polish

Apply two coats of polish. You should be able to cover the nail in three stokes, one on each side and then one in the middle.

Drying Time

Always allow your polish to dry thoroughly for several minutes before you apply the next coat. This will avoid the new coat from dragging on the surface of the previous coat and allow the next layer adhere better. Darker shades take longer to dry. Avoid fast drying polish. It does not last as long.

Top Coat

Once your nail polish has dried, apply a clear top coat to seal it. Continue to apply the

Top Coat daily to keep nails looking fresher longer. Remove with a nail polish remover that contains hydrating oils.

1. When will you file your nails?

2. Where do you start to buff your nails?

3. Why should you apply base coat and top coat while polishing your nails?

附录 A 常见外国女性的名字
Appendix A Common foreign females' name

名字	中译名	来源	含义
A			
Adela	爱德拉	德国	尊贵的,优雅的
Alice	艾丽斯	希腊	尊贵的,真诚的
Alma	爱玛	拉丁,英国	真情的,和善的
Alva	阿尔娃	拉丁	白皙的
Amy	艾米	法国	最心爱的人,可爱的
Ann	安妮	希伯来	优雅的,仁慈的上帝
Anna	安娜	希伯来	优雅
Athena	阿西娜	希腊	希腊神话中掌管智慧及战争的女神
B			
Barbara	芭芭拉	希腊	异乡人,异族人
Beatrice	碧翠丝	拉丁	为人祈福或使人快乐的女孩
Belinda	贝琳达	德国,意大利	有智慧又长寿的人
Bella	贝拉	拉丁	美丽的
Bess	贝丝	希伯来	上帝的誓约
Betty	贝蒂	希伯来	上帝的誓约
C			
Cara	卡拉	意大利	朋友,亲爱的人
Carol	卡萝	法国	欢唱,悦耳欢快的歌
Caroline	卡罗琳	条顿	骁勇、刚健和强壮的
Catherine	凯瑟琳	希腊	纯洁的人
Cathy	凯丝	希腊	凯瑟琳的昵称
Charlotte	夏洛特	法国	身体强健、女性化的
Cherry	切瑞	法国	仁慈,像樱桃般红润的人
Christine	克里斯汀	希腊	基督的追随者,门徒
Claire	克莱儿	拉丁	灿烂的,明亮的,聪明的
Clara	克莱拉	拉丁	明亮的,聪明的

Cora	科拉	希腊	处女,少女
Coral	卡洛儿	希腊,法国	珊瑚,彩石

D

Daisy	黛西	英国	雏菊
Dana	黛娜	希伯来	神的母亲,聪明且纯洁的
Daphne	黛芙妮	希腊神话	月桂树,桂冠
Debby	黛碧	希伯来	蜜蜂,蜂王,Deborah 的昵称
Deborah	德博拉	希伯来	蜜蜂,蜂王
Diana	戴安娜	拉丁	月亮女神
Donna	唐娜	拉丁	贵妇,淑女
Doris	多瑞丝	希腊	海洋女神
Dorothy	多罗斯	希腊	上帝的赠礼

E

Elizabeth	伊丽莎白	希伯来	上帝的誓约
Elma	艾尔玛	希腊	富爱心的人,亲切的
Elva	艾娃	斯堪的那维亚	神奇且智慧的
Emily	埃米莉	条顿,拉丁	勤勉奋发的,嗓音圆润的人
Emma	埃玛	条顿	祖先
Eve	伊芙	希伯来	赋予生命者,生灵之母

F

Fanny	芳妮	法国	自由之人
Florence	弗罗伦丝	塞尔特	开花的,美丽的

G

Georgia	乔治亚	希腊	农夫
Gill	姬儿	拉丁	少女
Gloria	葛罗瑞亚	拉丁	荣耀者,光荣者
Grace	葛瑞丝	英国,法国,拉丁	优雅的

H

Helen	海伦	希腊,拉丁	火把,光亮的
Hilda	希尔达	条顿	战斗,女战士
Hilary	希拉里	拉丁	快乐的
Honey	汉妮	英国	蜜糖,亲爱的人

I

Ida	埃达	德国	快乐的,勤奋的,富有的
Irene	艾琳	法国,拉丁	和平,和平女神
Iris	爱瑞丝	拉丁	彩虹女神,鸢尾花

Isabel	伊莎蓓尔	希伯来	上帝的誓约

J

Jane	简	希伯来,法国	少女
Janet	珍妮特	希伯来,法国	少女,上帝的恩赐
Joan	琼	法国	上帝仁慈的赠礼
Joanna	乔安娜	希伯来	上帝仁慈的赠礼
Josephine	约瑟芬	希伯来	多子女的女子
Judy	朱蒂	希伯来	赞美
Julia	朱莉娅	拉丁	头发柔软的
Julie	朱莉	希腊	柔和平静的女子
Juliet	朱丽叶	拉丁	头发柔软的,年轻的

K

Kama	卡玛	印度	爱之神
Karen	凯伦	希腊	纯洁
Katherine	凯瑟琳	希腊	纯洁的
Kitty	凯蒂	希腊	纯洁的

L

Laura	罗拉	拉丁	月桂树,胜利
Lillian	丽莲	希腊	百合花,纯洁的
Lisa	莉萨	希伯来	对神的奉献

M

Maggie	玛吉	拉丁	珍珠
Margaret	玛格丽特	拉丁	珍珠
Maria	玛丽亚	希伯来	圣洁的,圣母
Marian	玛丽安	希伯来,拉丁	优雅的
May	梅	拉丁	少女,五月
Merry	梅莉	英国	充满乐趣和笑声
Michelle	米歇尔	希伯来	紫菀花
Molly	茉莉	希伯来	海之女
Mona	莫娜	希腊	孤独,高贵
Monica	莫妮卡	拉丁	顾问

N

Nancy	南希	希伯来	优雅,温文尔雅
Nicole	妮可	希腊	胜利者

O

Olive	奥丽芙	拉丁	和平者,橄榄

Olivia	奥丽薇亚	拉丁	和平者,橄榄树

P

Pag	佩格	拉丁	珍珠
Pandora	潘多拉	希腊	火神用黏土做成的地上的第一个女人
Patricia	派翠西娅	拉丁	出身高贵的
Paula	波拉	拉丁	身材娇小玲珑者
Pearl	佩儿	拉丁	珍珠
Phoebe	菲碧	希腊	显赫的人,月之女神
Poppy	波比	拉丁	可爱的花朵

Q

Queena	奎娜	英国	高贵,贵族化的

R

Rachel	瑞切儿	希伯来	母羊或小羊,和善的
Rose	罗丝	拉丁	玫瑰花
Ruby	露比	法国	红宝石
Ruth	鲁思	希伯来	友谊,同情

S

Sabina	莎碧娜	拉丁	出身高贵的人
Sally	莎莉	希伯来	公主
Sarah	莎拉	希伯来	公主
Sheila	希拉	爱尔兰	少女,年轻女人,盲目的
Shirley	雪莉	英国	来自草地的
Sophia	苏菲亚	希腊	智慧的人
Susan	苏珊	希伯来	小百合
Susanna	苏珊娜	希伯来	百合花
Susie	苏西	希伯来	百合花

T

Tess	苔丝	法国	丰收

V

Verna	维娜	希腊	春天的美女,美丽的
Victoria	维多利亚	拉丁	胜利
Violet	维尔莉特	苏格兰,意大利	紫罗兰,谦虚
Virginia	维吉妮亚	拉丁	春天,欣欣向荣状

W

Wendy	温迪	条顿	有冒险精神的女孩

Z

Zara	左拉	希伯来	黎明
Zona	若娜	拉丁	黎明

附录 B 中外节日英汉对照
Appendix B Chinese and Foreign Festivals

阳历 **Solar Calendar**

1月1日	元旦	New Year's Day
2月14日	情人节	Valentine's Day
3月8日	国际妇女节	International Women's Day
3月12日	中国植树节	China Arbor Day
4月1日	愚人节	April Fools' Day
4月5日	清明节	Tomb-sweeping Day
5月1日	国际劳动节	International Labor Day
5月4日	中国青年节	Chinese Youth Day
5月12日	国际护士节	International Nurse Day
6月1日	国际儿童节	International Children's Day
7月1日	中国共产党诞生日	Anniversary of the Founding of the Chinese Communist Party
8月1日	中国人民解放军建军节	Chinese People's Liberation Army Day
8月12日	国际青年节	International Youth Day
9月10日	中国教师节	Chinese Teachers' Day
10月1日	中华人民共和国国庆节	National Day of the People's Republic of China
10月5日	世界教师日（联合国教科文组织确立）	World Teachers' Day
10月31日	万圣节前夕	Halloween
11月1日	万圣节	All Saints Day
12月1日	世界艾滋病日	World AIDS Day
12月24日	圣诞节前夕	Christmas Eve
12月25日	圣诞节	Christmas Day

复活节	Easter
（春分月圆后的第一个星期日，有可能是 3 月 22 日至 4 月 25 日的任一天）	
5 月第二个星期日　母亲节	Mother's Day
6 月第三个星期日　父亲节	Father's Day
10 月的第二个星期一　加拿大感恩节	Canadians' Thanksgiving Day
11 月第四个星期四　美国感恩节	Americans' Thanksgiving Day

农历	**Lunar Calendar**
农历正月初一　春节	the Spring Festival
农历正月十五　元宵节	Lantern Festival
农历五月初五　端午节	the Dragon Boat Festival
农历七月初七　七夕节（中国情人节）	Double-Seventh Day
农历八月十五　中秋节	the Mid-Autumn Festival
农历九月初九　重阳节	the Double Ninth Festival

附录 C 背景知识和网站链接
Appendix C Background Information and Web Links

1. 自然美容养生馆　Natural Beauty Salon
http://wenku.baidu.com/view/cb93cdd5360cba1aa811dae6.html

2. 皮肤护理产品　Skin Care Products
http://www.ladyburd.com/category.php?id=2

3. 化妆品的标识　Labels of Cosmetics
http://whatscookingamerica.net/HealthBeauty/CosmeticLabeling.htmWhatare Cosmetics?

4. 防晒和晒伤　Sunscreen VS Sunblock
http://hubpages.com/hub/Sunscreen-VS-Sunblock

5. 如何在电话中说话得体　How to Speak Nicely on the Phone
http://www.wikihow.com/Speak-Nicely-on-the-Phone

6. 手机使用礼仪　Mobile Phone Etiquette
http://edu.qq.com/a/20101206/000339.htm

7. 皮肤的种类　Types of Skin
http://beauty.about.com/od/skinflaws/a/skintypes.htm

8. 长粉刺的原因　What Causes Acne
http://www.proactiv.com/aboutacne/howacnehappens.php

9. 日常清洁的程序　Practice a Regular Cleansing Routine
http://www.tingroom.com/lesson/meirongss/88358.html

10. 脸部按摩　Facial Massage
http://chino.expertmassagetherapy.com/post/2010/10/18/Facial-Massage-Chino-CA.aspx

11. 眼睛浮肿的自然修复方法　Natural Remedies for Puffy Eyes
http://video.about.com/beauty/Remedies-for-Puffy-Eyes.htm

12. 怎样找穴位　How to Find a Point
http://www.acupressureinstitute.com/articles/a-how_to_find_a_point.html

13. 指压的介绍　Introduction to Acupressure
http://www.acupressureinstitute.com/articles/a-introduction_to_acupressure.html

14. 背部按摩　Back Massage
http://www.easyvigour.net.nz/backpain/h_BackMassage.htm

15. SPA 疗法　SPA treatment
http://en.wikipedia.org/wiki/Spa

16. 自然疗法　Natural Therapies

http://www.naturaltherapypages.com.au/article/What_is_a_Natural_Therapy

17. 新娘妆的 10 个技巧　10 Tips of Bridal Make-up

http://www.kekenet.com/read/200912/92723_10.shtml

18. 美甲　Manicure

http://www.nciku.cn/conversation/detailview?convseq=2991&categoryLanguage=zh

19. 指甲护理技巧——自然美甲　Nail Care Tips-Beautiful Nature Nails

http://www.nailcareguide.com/

参 考 文 献
References

［1］中国就业培训技术指导中心.美容师（技师）[M].北京：中国劳动社会保障出版社，2006.
［2］华立图书编委会.实用美容英语[M].台北：华立图书股份有限公司，1997.
［3］熊蕊,陈丽君.面部护理技术[M].武汉：华中科技大学出版社,2017.
［4］熊蕊,王艳,梁超兰.身体护理技术[M].武汉：华中科技大学出版社,2017.

本书写作过程中使用了部分图片，在此向这些图片的版权所有人表示诚挚的谢意！由于客观原因，我们无法联系到你。请相关版权所有人与出版社联系，出版社将按照国家相关规定和行业标准支付稿酬。